How Sportsmen Saved the World

The Unsung Conservation Efforts of Hunters and Anglers

E. DONNALL THOMAS JR.

LYONS PRESS
Guilford, Connecticut
An imprint of Globe Pequot Press

Lyons Press is an imprint of Globe Pequot Press.

Text design: Libby Kingsbury
Layout: Lisa Reneson
Project editor: John Burbidge

Library of Congress Cataloging-in-Publication Data
Thomas, E. Donnall, 1948-
  How sportsmen saved the world : the unsung conservation efforts of hunters and anglers / E. Donnall Thomas Jr.
      p. cm.
  Includes bibliographical references and index.
  ISBN 978-1-59921-522-8
  1. Hunting—United States—History. 2. Hunters—United States.
3. Wildlife conservationists—United States. I. Title.
  SK41.T44 2010
  333.95'416—dc22
                                        2009025452
Printed in the United States of America

10 9 8 7 6 5 4 3 2 1

To my parents, E. Donnall Thomas Sr. and Dorothy Thomas

CONTENTS

Acknowledgments

In addition to individuals identified directly in the text, I wish to thank the following people for their assistance: Mike Beagle, Anthony Hauck, John Hoffman, Laura Houseseal, Butch Huffaker, Chris Hunt, Kirby Kohler, Terry Lonner, Katie McKillip, Geoff Mullins, Andrea and Doug Peacock, David Petersen, Paul Queneau, Jeanine Richards, Tony Schoonen, and Tom Stivers.

Special thanks go to Dr. Valerius Geist, Bart James, Maurice Nichols, Jim Posewitz, and the late Jim Range, each of whom provided more freely of their time than I had a right to ask.

Finally, Allen Jones of Lyons Press deserves special recognition. In addition to countless helpful suggestions during the editing process, Allen conceived the idea for this book and provided its title. I'm not sure why he didn't just write it himself; he certainly would have done an excellent job.

PREFACE

This book's thesis is simple and logical: Faced with human development's ever-increasing demands upon habitat, wildlife today needs advocates more than ever before.

When wildlife advocates work together, wildlife wins; when they bicker, wildlife loses.

Outdoor sports—hunting and, to a lesser extent, angling—are receiving ever-increasing levels of criticism from other elements of the wildlife advocacy community, often based on the apparently obvious fact that these activities are harmful to wildlife.

This "apparently obvious" fact is quite incorrect. The historical record shows that North American sportsmen have been at the forefront of almost every significant advance in the protection of the continent's wildlife. These efforts have led to a system of wildlife and habitat management superior to that in any other region in the world.

If wildlife advocates who do not hunt or fish acknowledged this record, we might be able to stop fighting with each other and invest our time, money, and political influence where it belongs: in the defense of wildlife and the places it calls home.

That last consideration is all that really matters to me. I have spent most of my sixty years engaged in a wide variety of outdoor activities, including hunting and fishing. I recognize that many members of our society disapprove of some of these interests, and that this disapproval may be strong enough to interfere with potential friendships or lead to unpleasant confrontations. I'm quite willing to accept that disapproval without comment—as long as it doesn't interfere with what really counts. When an anti-hunting group files a frivolous, biologically unjustified lawsuit against a regulatory agency, both sides waste countless measures of time and money, assets that could have been employed to help buttress wildlife's defense against what really threatens it: loss of habitat. I'm tired of it.

In support of this thesis, we will examine the lives and work of the giants in the history of wildlife conservation. Some, like Theodore Roosevelt and Aldo Leopold, are well known, if only for their work in other fields. Others, like George Bird Grinnell and Ding Darling, may be unknown even to lifelong outdoorsmen (which should tell us something about the shabby way we treat our own history). All were sportsmen—hunters and anglers who recognized the essential relationship between sound wildlife management and the future of their sport.

We'll also look at sportsman-driven wildlife organizations past and present, analyzing their contributions to the American conservation movement. Finally, we'll look at the bottom line—species saved from the brink of extinction, habitat protected from development, policies designed to safeguard wildlife into the future—and the essential role sportsmen played in those developments.

No one concerned with the role of outdoor sport in modern society is free of personal bias. I have tried to present the historical record as clearly and accurately as possible, and to identify my own opinions as such. As a demonstration of good faith, I have even included segments on issues in which sportsmen have *not* always acted as ideal wildlife advocates might have. Hopefully this will reassure readers familiar with my work elsewhere in the outdoor press, where I have never hesitated to hold sportsmen's feet to the fire when I felt they deserved it.

In the end, I feel confident that the facts will speak for themselves.

Since I grew up in a family in which men and women enjoyed the outdoors on equal terms, I regret the gender-specific "sportsmen" of the title, for which I could produce no reasonable alternative. And the fact that the individuals profiled in the historical segment of the text are all male simply reflects the customs of the times in which those events took place. I recognize that an ever increasing number of women hunt and fish today, welcome this development, and eagerly anticipate the contributions these sports-*women* will make to the future of wildlife in America.

Part One

Wildlife in America: A Brief History

Back from the Brink

One April day some years back, my wife, Lori, and I spent the afternoon hiking in a long, lazy circle through the meadows and pine ridges near our central Montana home. I was carrying a longbow, and we were looking for wild turkeys. Every time we reached a new overlook, we'd pause to call down into the canyons below, all of which initially remained stubbornly silent in the face of my plaintive yelps. But after a long winter's worth of more time indoors than either of us cared for, that hardly mattered. With a couple of dropped mule deer antlers in my backpack and the location of some September elk rubs fixed in my brain, it was hard to call the afternoon a failure despite the absence of our ostensible quarry.

As we began to work our way down the ridge that would lead us back to our camp, Lori suddenly froze midstride. Her ears are younger than mine, and they've endured a lot less exposure to shotguns and airplane engines. I learned years ago that when she thinks she's heard something I haven't, I'd better stop and pay attention. "I thought I heard a hen," she whispered, pointing down into the yawning canyon ahead of us. Moments later I heard a yelp myself, but it sounded so far off that it was impossible to localize its source above the sigh of the mountain breeze.

As I considered our options, I instinctively moved toward a little cluster of immature pines at the edge of the field so we would have access to cover if we needed it in a hurry—a prescient move, as events soon proved. Then I heard the haunting, unmistakable sound of a gobble.

To move along the rim of the hill in an attempt to localize the bird would run the risk of spooking him, so I licked my diaphragm call out of my face mask and into my mouth and cut loose with a brisk series of yelps. The response could not have been more dramatic. The sound of my own last call had barely cleared my lips when a thunderous gobble issued in reply, and the rapid sequence of responses from the tom made it obvious that he was inbound on the run. Diving into the little stand of evergreen trees, I quickly dug a length of camo netting from my day pack and stretched it across a gap in the pines while Lori crawled ten yards out across the grass and set up a pair of silhouette decoys. She barely had time to retreat back into the cover when the gobbler appeared over the lip of the hill.

I've spent decades calling in creatures varying in size from mallard to moose. Watching a mature gobbler respond to my calls excites me every bit as much as bugling in a bull elk. In this case, my choice of weapon only exaggerated the tension, for I had decided many seasons earlier to hunt turkeys exclusively with my bow. Because of their constant alertness and superior vision, wild turkeys are as challenging as any quarry a bow hunter will face in North America.

As the gobbler closed relentlessly toward the fifteen-yard range I needed, it seemed that a miracle was about to take place. The miracle wasn't just that I was about to kill a big gobbler with a longbow. The miracle was that there were turkeys to hunt in the first place.

The largest of all gallinaceous birds, the wild turkey, *Meleagris gallopavo,* is native to North America. While the legend of the first Thanksgiving has been subjected to modern skepticism, the turkey was clearly an important traditional food source for Native Americans on the eastern seaboard, where early European colonists not only began to hunt it for subsistence, but eventually domesticated it and shipped tame versions back across the Atlantic as early as the 1600s. (The turkey is one of only two species of domestic birds to originate in North America. The Muscovy duck, native to Central and South America, is the second.)

A spectacular species in appearance and habit as well as size, the wild turkey quickly captured the imagination of the new American republic. John James Audubon chose the turkey as the subject of the first plate in his monumental *Birds of America*. While the story that Ben Franklin lobbied the Continental Congress to make the turkey rather than the bald eagle our national emblem isn't quite true, it has some basis in fact. In a letter to his daughter written in 1784, Franklin launched into a long, derogatory tirade against the bald eagle before suggesting this alternative: "The turkey is in Comparison a much more respectable bird and withal a true original native of North America . . . a Bird of Courage who would not hesitate to attack a Grenadier of the British Guards."

I'm not sure Franklin had *all* his facts straight; if so, I should have been wearing a red military uniform during all those spring excursions into the turkey cover.

It's really impossible to arrive at an accurate estimate of the turkey population's size in pre-colonial America, though the birds certainly numbered in the millions. Despite their legendary wariness, those numbers began to drop soon after Europeans arrived on the eastern seaboard, as a result of several factors. Although poorly suited to killing big game, the primitive firearms early colonists carried were adequate for turkeys, especially when combined with Native American hunting skills, which the colonists quickly began to acquire. Turkeys soon became an important market commodity as well. Shortly after the *Mayflower* colonists arrived, William Bradford assigned men the specific task of hunting wild turkeys, and a turkey was worth four shillings throughout most of the English-speaking colonies during the 1600s. Market demand also motivated skilled Indian hunters to do what they had never done before: kill more turkeys than they could smoke or consume on the spot.

The impact on turkey populations was abrupt. In his 1672 tract *New England's Rarities Discovered*, John Josselyn wrote, "I have also seen threescore of young Turkies on the side of a march, sunning of themselves in a morning beside, but this was thirty years since, the English and the Indians having now destroyed the breed, so that 'tis rare to meet with a wild Turkey in the Woods."

The subsequent near-extinction of the bison may make a more dramatic and better-known story, but it's instructive to realize that the wild turkey, an intrinsically more adaptable species, was in trouble two centuries before that—no doubt simply because European colonists and their firearms were able to reach them sooner.

Turkeys originally inhabited thirty-nine states; by 1920, they had completely disappeared from eighteen of them. Turkey numbers reached a nationwide low of some thirty thousand during the Depression era. Most accounts of that near-disaster blame hunting for the population crash, and that's at least partly true. However, the unregulated hunting that almost eliminated the wild turkey was for subsistence and the market, as distinct from the modern practice of sport hunting. Furthermore, habitat loss was likely an even more important cause of the turkey's decline. America's rapid western expansion resulted in the sudden destruction of vast tracts of their preferred mature hardwood habitat, a phenomenon that had profound effects on another more unfortunate species: the passenger pigeon.

It's sobering to realize how close we came to bringing one of the world's most spectacular avian species to extinction. But there's also some good news, and I was celebrating it that spring day in the central Montana foothills. The 1937 Federal Aid in Wildlife Restoration Act—which sportsmen conceived and lobbied for heavily—created a source of funding for projects designed, among other things, to bring the wild turkey back from the brink. The actual dollars came from a federal excise tax on guns, ammunition, and other sporting goods that continues to fund important wildlife projects to this day—and which still ultimately derive from American hunters and anglers (the analogous Dingell-Johnson bill created a similar excise tax on angling equipment in 1950). State game departments and private parties began to work on habitat restoration, and wild turkey stocks were reintroduced throughout their original native range and beyond.

New York State, where I spent my early childhood, offers an illustrative example of this wildlife success story. I spent as many hours in the woods as I could from the time I was old enough to walk, and can guarantee that there were no wild turkeys in Otsego County when I was growing up there in the 1950s. In fact, the last recorded observation of a native wild turkey in New York prior to reintroduction came in 1844. A few birds occasionally wandered across the Pennsylvania border into southern New York, but self-sustaining permanent populations weren't established until the New York Department of Environmental Conservation (NYDEC) began transplanting eastern turkeys to the state in 1957. The results were spectacular, which just goes to show what habitat restoration and appropriately regulated hunting can accomplish. In 1960 the NYDEC estimated the state's wild turkey population at two thousand; by 1990 it had risen to sixty-five thousand, and it's much higher today despite, or more properly *because of*, a robust turkey-hunting season in New York.

Montana, where I've spent most of my adult life, offers an interesting historical contrast, even if the net result is similarly gratifying. Originally, there were no wild turkeys in Montana. They are one of the few important native game species absent from Lewis and Clark's records of their passage through the state but thriving along the Corps of Discovery's route today. On an 1833 hunting expedition, the German sportsman Prince Maximilian reported eastern turkeys in what is now South Dakota, but no farther west. He postulated that the terrain was too open for the eastern subspecies, and I think he was right.

At the same time wild turkeys were being reintroduced in New York, Montana's Department of Fish, Wildlife & Parks (called the Department of Fish & Game back then) transplanted the first Merriam turkeys to the state. With a home range in the arid Southwest, the Merriam subspecies seemed best suited for the open habitat Maximilian commented on a century before. I can see the site of that 1954 release in the Judith Mountains from my home today. Despite initial uncertainty about their future, the turkeys provided a pleasant surprise, dispersing to occupy diverse habitats ranging from timbered ridges in the mountains to cottonwood bottoms on the plains in the state's eastern half. Those introductions were funded with hunters' dollars, and sportsmen frequently volunteered their time and assistance to the transplant efforts.

Montana held its first limited turkey season in 1959. The West lacked the established turkey-hunting traditions familiar east of the Mississippi, and it took most Montana hunters years to figure out the game. Nowadays, however, thousands eagerly anticipate Montana's spring turkey season as a welcome opportunity to get back in the woods after a long, confining winter.

The success of Montana's Merriam turkeys raises an important biological question: If they can thrive here now, why hadn't they naturally populated the area by migrating north from their native range in Colorado? The answer must have something to do with the way human settlement has changed the landscape. I think it lies in the character of Montana's frequently brutal winters, which even today determine turkey population numbers to a far greater extent than all predators combined, including human hunters. Prior to settlement, Montana winter weather resulted in too much snow for turkeys to survive. Nowadays, the birds migrate down the mountains to winter in cattle feedlots during periods of heavy snow.

By the time I had an arrow on the string, the gobbler had closed upon the decoys. When he pivoted in full strut, I took advantage of the eclipse provided by his extended tail feathers to draw and release. The broadhead struck him at the base of the wing quartering away, and he tore back across the open meadow only to collapse in plain sight. As we closed upon the fallen bird, I felt briefly overwhelmed by the sense of amazement I always experience when I manage to kill a turkey with sticks and string. I also realized how utterly lucky our afternoon's hunt would have looked to any of my experienced southern turkey-hunting friends. The list of elementary turkey-hunting rules we'd broken seemed longer than the list of those we'd obeyed. But the bottom line remained immune to challenge: We were walking out of the woods with a turkey.

Surveys consistently show that the non-hunting public is more disposed to view sportsmen favorably when hunters eat what they shoot. No cause for alarm on my part—I *do* eat what I shoot and consider the preparation of game for the table as important as the hunt itself. This is especially true in the case of the wild turkey, a culinary delight whose reputation has suffered needlessly at novice hands due to the usual scourge of inept wild game preparation: overcooking. I had better things in mind for this bird, and as we hiked back toward camp, Lori and I made a deliberate detour through a cottonwood bottom to search for the missing ingredient necessary to turn fantasy into a special dinner—fresh wild morels.

When we arrived back at our tent with our mission accomplished, our whole afternoon felt miraculous. Calling in the tom had been exciting, the shot gratifying, the mushrooms an unexpected bonus. But the real miracle was the product of the effort by the hundreds of thousands of hunters and their allies who brought the wild turkey back from the brink. From a nationwide population low of thirty thousand birds in the 1930s, their numbers have increased to a robust seven million today. Wild turkey populations are now established in every state except Alaska. While hunters funded their reintroduction and habitat restoration, the birds are there for all to enjoy—photographers, birders, or casual observers who simply enjoy watching turkeys strut and listening to gobbles echo through the woods every spring.

Despite their crucial role in such dramatic wildlife success stories, hunters have become pariahs in many segments of America's increasingly urbanized society. This development has been startlingly abrupt. We began as a nation of frontiersmen and hunters, and as such developed the individual skills necessary to defeat the larger, better-equipped British army in the Revolutionary War. As recently as one generation ago, Ernest Hemingway was an icon in popular American culture, and Hollywood celebrities and politicians openly discussed their hunting experiences in public. The greening of America logically should have led to an increased public appreciation of the role hunters and anglers have played in restoring crucial wildlife populations and habitat. So why the disconnection between a century's record of advocacy on behalf of fish and game and the popular misperception that sportsmen actually threaten the wildlife and wild places they have fought to restore?

This volume's primary mission is to document objectively the extent and importance of just what hunters and anglers have done for wildlife. When members of the non-hunting public delight in the sight of wild turkeys strutting in a field next spring, those observers should know where the turkeys came from and why they're here today.

THE GARDEN OF EDEN

H*omo sapiens sapiens* (wise, *wise* man, a flattering name our species does not always deserve) evolved as a hunter, a role our species has played instinctively throughout most of its existence. Hunting played a crucial role in the development of numerous traits that define us as a species, including the prehensile thumb, the origins of speech and language, basic social institutions that distinguish us from other primates, and intelligence itself.

In a paper delivered at a 1966 symposium on the subject of man the hunter, academic anthropologist William Laughlin wrote: "Hunting played the dominant role in transforming a bipedal ape into a tool-using and tool-making man who communicated by means of speech and expressed a complex culture in the infinite number of ways now known to us. The evolutionary importance of hunting can be demonstrated by a combination of nutritional, psychological, and anatomical (including neurophysiological) aspects of our contemporary behavior, with the fossil and archeological record, and with primate comparisons."

And as Charles Bergman notes in *Orion's Legacy*: "Hunting is wrapped in the swirls of our DNA, and woven in the adaptations of culture. It is a natural and evolutionary pressure, the most important in all of humanity's evolutionary adaptations."

Those adaptations occurred over millennia. On a more recent time scale, hunting remained an essential means of life support for many human populations prior to the Industrial Revolution. Neither the "Native" Americans who first populated our continent by way of the Bering Sea land bridge nor the early European immigrants who crossed the Atlantic some fifteen thousand years later could have survived in their brave new world without hunting, which they considered an acceptable practice for the most basic reason of all: It was essential to human survival.

Neither its necessity nor its universal acceptance endure, two facts no doubt closely related. Walt Disney's 1942 animated feature *Bambi* initiated decades' worth of media characterization of hunters as villains. (Bambi is an interesting story on its own. Austrian novelist Felix Saltern's original story had more to do with Freudian conflict than hunting, and its first English translation from the German was done by Whitaker Chambers, of Cold War spydom infamy.) The publication of *Animal Liberation* by the Australian philosopher Peter Singer in 1975 created an organized intellectual framework for the visceral animosity hunting evoked among many animal lovers. A major American news magazine subsequently posed a blunt question on its cover: *Should Hunting Be Banned?*

This kind of anti-hunting sentiment largely derived from moral and social concerns: Is hunting *right*? Is it an activity in which civilized people should still engage? These are perfectly legitimate questions that by their very nature defy easy answers.

The publication of Rachel Carson's *Silent Spring* in 1962 was to ecological awareness as *Bambi* was to the defense of the cute and cuddly: a seminal media event that irrevocably changed America's attitude toward wildlife and its habitat. In contrast to Disney, however, Carson's thesis was supported by fact rather than raw emotion. Growing up in the 1950s, I never heard the term *ecology*. Now that the admirable greening of America has turned ecology into a universally recognized concept, it's hard to recall the skepticism and outright vilification that greeted Carson's original work.

Although she died unvindicated at an early age, Carson had set in motion an important notion in our collective conscience: The most technically advanced nation on earth was destroying its environment and wildlife heritage, and we damn well ought to start doing something about it. And one of the most important corollaries of Carson's thesis went unstated. By 1962 the Bambi generation had already begun to misidentify sportsmen as the principal threat to American wildlife. Carson showed that the real threat wasn't coming from hunters, but from a technology-obsessed society gone awry.

Even so, hunting became a public relations casualty of the environmental consciousness Carson's work eventually aroused. After all, hunters killed wildlife, and wildlife needed to be saved (true-true-unrelated, to invoke the old multiple choice test question format). The obvious legitimacy of the underlying concern aroused fresh skepticism about the propriety of hunting, even among thoughtful individuals capable of seeing past the raw emotionalism of *Bambi*. Attempts by the responsible outdoor community to convince an increasingly skeptical public of its role in wildlife habitat conservation evoked unfortunate echoes of the Vietnam-era dictum about destroying villages in order to save them. Hunters killed the very things that needed saving. What could be more obviously wrong?

But in contrast to these moral and societal questions about hunting, the ecological and scientific arguments for and against hunting are subject to objective validation, historical and contemporary. The essential issue becomes: Are modern sporting practices good or bad for wildlife and its future? I believe the question can be answered in concrete ways that questions about animal rights cannot. And if wildlife is better off with hunting than without it, moral and societal objections to hunting can be treated as what they are: legitimate matters of personal belief that form a poor basis for public policy.

An examination of the status of wildlife in early America offers a logical point of beginning.

Accurate inventories of American wildlife resources prior to the Revolution are obviously difficult to come by. Biological science of all kinds was in its infancy; the terms *wildlife biology* and *ecology* had yet to be coined. Few if any resources were available for formal study. Huge portions of the continent remained unknown to colonial observers, and their Native inhabitants kept few written records.

Fish and game were certainly plentiful in the New World when the first Europeans arrived. Anecdotal descriptions by early explorers and colonists consistently reflect both their startling abundance and the importance of these resources to the lives of early settlers. Exploring the Saint Lawrence River in 1545, Jacques Cartier reported "a great store of Stags, Deere, Beares, and other like sorts of beasts as Connies, Hares, Martens, Foxes, Otters, Beavers, Weasels, Badgers and Rats, and exceedingly great and diverse other sorts of wild beasts." When the *Mayflower* arrived in Provincetown Harbor in November 1620, John Bradford found it full of ducks and geese, "the greatest store of fowl that ever we saw." And while details of the first Thanksgiving remain open to question, Bradford also noted "a good store of wild turkeys" that fall. In his *New English Caanan,* Thomas Morton, renegade founder of the delightfully heretical Merry Mount colony and one of the New World's first successful market hunters, described "Millions of Turtle doves" and "Fowles in abundance."

It remains difficult to translate such descriptions into accurate numbers even in the case of important, readily observed species like the white-tailed deer. Once wildlife in early America stopped being a pure subsistence staple and became a commodity, commercial records allowed at least some objective supplementation of firsthand accounts of abundance. And they confirm the presence of tremendous numbers of white-tailed deer in pre-revolutionary America.

Royal Customs Service records show that 600,000 deer hides were shipped to England from Savannah for the British leather industry from 1755 to 1773. Another 30,000 to 40,000 were shipped annually from each of several other southern ports. During the 1750s, deer hides exported to England from Florida exceeded the value of all other trade commodities from the area combined. In 1763 alone, Virginia and Maryland sent 25,000 British pounds' worth of deer hides across the Atlantic, and

Pennsylvania shipped another 50,000 pounds' worth. Even after a century and a half of subsistence exploitation, the size of the deer herd necessary to sustain this commercial output must have been staggering.

A number of modern authorities have proposed "best guess" estimates of pre-colonial populations of large game animals based on various research methods including the study of archeological sites and careful review of firsthand accounts by early settlers and explorers. While recognizing their inherent limitations, these analyses still provide a useful frame of reference. In 1909 E. T. Seton offered one of the first such studies and came up with the following numbers for the continental United States: bison, 50 to 60 million; pronghorn, 40 million; white-tailed deer, 20 million; mule deer, 10 million; elk, 10 million. In 1978 F. H. Wagner suggested the following numbers for eleven western states: bison, 10 to 50 million; pronghorn, 10 to 15 million; mule deer, 5 million; elk, 2 million; bighorn sheep, 1 million. The numbers are not immediately comparable because of the limited geographic range in Wagner's work. Most modern biologists consider Seton's numbers liberal and Wagner's conservative. The truth likely lies somewhere between.

The wide range of variation in these estimated numbers gives rise to a curious but predictable modern phenomenon: selective citation. For example, different sources present pre-colonial antelope population estimates that vary from five million to sixty million. These numbers are often presented as established fact with no mention of the uncertainties or the range of expert opinion, and the number chosen often reflects the agenda of the group presenting it. Anti-hunting organizations often present high initial estimates to dramatize the extent of the animals' decline at human hands (just as they choose *low* figures for current population estimates). John Le Carré's splendid fictional British spymaster George Smiley neatly summarized the moral of this story when he pointed out that information is no more valuable than its source.

Large ungulates are not the only species relevant to this discussion. Early American colonists settled near the coast for obvious reasons, and fish were as critical to their survival as game. Contemporary records clearly document their abundance. Highly prized as game fish today, striped bass were so plentiful that early colonists used them for fertilizer. In fact, the Massachusetts Bay Colony's 1639 proclamation, "And it is forbidden to all men, after the 20th of next month, to employ any codd or basse fish for manuring the ground," represents the colonies' first attempt to regulate the harvest of wildlife. Bluefish represented another important marine staple. The 1794 *Collections of the Massachusetts Historical Society* notes, "From the first coming of the English to Nantucket, a large, fat fish called the Bluefish was caught in great abundance all around the island."

Teeming with salmon and sturgeon, the colonies' freshwater rivers were as rich a source of subsistence as the sea. No species was more important to America's early economy or the nutritional needs of its inhabitants than the shad. In 1686 William Penn, during a rare visit to the colony that bore his name, observed: "Shads are excellent fish and of the bigness of our Carp. They are so plentiful that Captain Smyth's Overseer at the Skulkil, drew 600 and odd at one Draught; 300 is no wonder; 100 familiarly."

Our ability to appreciate the continent's wildlife resources took a qualitative turn in May 1804, when the Corps of Discovery set off up the Missouri River toward the distant Pacific. Conceived by Thomas Jefferson in a remarkable example of what a later president termed "the vision thing," the expedition's immediate mandate was to chart territory newly acquired through the Louisiana Purchase. However, Jefferson, a true Renaissance man and natural historian in his own right, recognized the importance of describing, classifying, and collecting the flora and fauna of the new American frontier, and he made that responsibility an imperative while the expedition was in its earliest planning stages. He could not have picked better men for the job.

Meriwether Lewis was a captain in the Regular Army when Jefferson began grooming him to lead the Corps of Discovery. His principal qualifications were courage, character, and experience with Indians on the frontier. Jefferson also noted that Lewis had made "a great mass of accurate observations" about the wildlife around his Virginia home, not, alas, "under their scientific forms, but so as that he will readily seize what is new in the country he passes through." William Clark, who had resigned his commission in the army several years previously, shared similar basic qualifications plus one: He was a trained cartographer.

In retrospect, it's easy to fault both men's lack of formal training in biological science. However, the field was populated by amateurs at the time, to the extent it was populated at all. If the young nation had better qualified biologists, they almost certainly lacked the wilderness survival experience Lewis and Clark enjoyed, skills that would prove more important than "book learning" to the expedition's scientific mission in the long run. What the expedition's leaders lacked in formal training they made up for in traits critical to any student of natural history: intense curiosity and astute powers of observation.

Their patchy scientific résumés notwithstanding, events proved the wisdom of Jefferson's choices. By the time the expedition returned to Saint Louis in September 1806, its leaders' meticulous field notes contained the first written descriptions of 122 species of animals and 178 species of plants previously unknown to Western science (although no doubt widely familiar to the Native Americans who inhabited the expedition's route). While two centuries of scrutiny have called a few of those descriptions and rough classifications into question, the degree to which they have withstood the test of time remains remarkable. After living much of my life near the expedition's route, studying the *Journals* carefully and comparing them to my own observations in the wild, I can summarize my own attitude toward this remarkable record of early American wildlife in three words: I believe it.

That confidence makes the abundance of wildlife the *Journals* describe all the more remarkable. On September 17, 1804, Lewis made the following notes in what is now eastern South Dakota: "This scenery, already rich, pleasing, and beautiful, was still further heightened by rich herds of buffalo, elk, deer, and antelope, which we saw in every direction feeding on the hills and plains.

I do not think I exaggerate when I estimate the number of buffalo which could be comprehended in one view to be 3,000." Similar descriptions recur throughout their long passage across the plains.

In contrast to some later visitors who found the impulse to engage in pointless slaughter irresistible, the expedition's leaders took a practical, restrained position with regard to the abundance of game, as indicated in Lewis's note of April 27, 1805, at the confluence of the Missouri and Yellowstone Rivers: "Although the game is very abundant and gentle, we only kill as much as is necessary for food. I believe that two good hunters could easily supply a regiment with provisions."

This enlightened attitude notwithstanding, the expedition went through a lot of game for purely utilitarian reasons. They had no ready source of calories and protein other than the barely palatable dried staples they had brought along and what vegetables they could barter from the Indians. Engaged in vigorous physical labor from dawn until dark, the three dozen members of the expedition consumed an estimated nine pounds of venison per person per day, and the ease with which the hunters, armed with nothing but primitive flintlocks, obtained it provides additional evidence of the abundant wildlife they encountered. On November 19, 1804, near Fort Mandan, Clark casually reported, "Our pirogue of hunters arrived with 32 deer, 12 elk, and a buffalo." The following February, he wrote, "He (Lewis) hunted two days; killed 36 deer and 14 elk." Wildlife populations that allowed such harvests with primitive weapons must have been staggering.

We will never be able to arrive at a precise inventory of wildlife resources in North America prior to the era of European colonization and eventual exploitation. The tools modern biologists use to count noses did not exist, the distances between the field and centers of study were vast, and means of recording and communicating observations were limited. If the inferences drawn from eyewitness accounts, archeological records, and secondary sources like commercial harvest data conflicted, best guess estimates such as the widely cited figure of twenty to forty million white-tailed deer in pre-colonial America would be even broader in range and more suspect in their accuracy.

However, it's difficult to find information from any of these various sources that suggests anything other than an abundance of wildlife. While one can legitimately argue the exact numbers, the impression of plenty seems universal.

And it was not destined to last.

THE FALL: AMERICAN WILDLIFE IN THE NINETEENTH CENTURY

Anyone inclined toward complacency about wildlife should take a hard look at what happened here in America during the century that followed the descriptions Lewis and Clark recorded in their *Journals*.

By the beginning of the twentieth century, America's white-tailed deer population had fallen to 300,000 from the estimated 20 to 40 million cited earlier. Pronghorn antelope numbers had dropped from 40 million to 20,000, and bison went from 30 to 60 million to scattered bands on protected ranges. The plains grizzlies Lewis and Clark encountered regularly were gone, along with the "big-horned animal" (the Audubon subspecies of bighorn sheep) they encountered so frequently along the breaks of the Missouri. The elk that swarmed along their route had declined from a pre-colonial population of millions to fewer than 50,000 in remote areas that represented a small fraction of their original range. While the accuracy of these initial estimates is subject to question, the nadir figures are relatively precise in comparison. Unfortunately, our ability to count wildlife almost came too late to matter.

Big game animals were not the only species affected. In 1839 the Massachusetts Zoological and Botanical Survey reported, "The Concord shad have almost entirely disappeared, their ascent having been cut off by dams." The last wild passenger pigeon was killed on March 24, 1900, in Pike County, Ohio, as if to usher in the new century.

Understanding what happened and why, and how closely we came to driving not just the passenger pigeon but dozens of crucial indigenous fish and game species to the brink of extinction and beyond, is essential to anyone interested in wildlife today, whether they hunt and fish or not. This near-disaster establishes the importance of two themes that will recur throughout this book: the central role of habitat preservation in the future of wildlife, and the critical distinction between the commercial exploitation of fish and game on one hand and regulated sport hunting and angling on the other, as illustrated by two important examples.

The Destruction of the Bison

Few large animals illustrate the disaster that befell American wildlife during the nineteenth century as poignantly as the American bison, *Bison bison*. (Although widely known as buffalo, the species, derived from Eurasian progenitors of cattle and oxen that crossed the Bering Sea land bridge into the New World, are not related to the true buffalo of Africa and southern Asia.)

Eurasian immigrants themselves, Native Americans had depended upon bison for millennia as a critical source of food, clothing, shelter, and fuel. The continent's oldest known human artifact, the Folsom point, was found embedded in a bison bone shown by carbon dating to be 10,000 years old. In the majority of pre-Columbian archeological sites within the bison's historic range, bison bones outnumber those of all other ungulates combined. But because of low human population density and inefficient means of harvest, Native Americans posed no overall biological threat to the bison during the first several thousand years they shared habitat together on the Great Plains, despite the animals' importance to the Indians' survival.

However, while unregulated slaughter by white market hunters was certainly the proximate cause of the bison population's collapse during the late nineteenth century, evidence suggests that buffalo numbers had already started to drop significantly prior to the time of westward American expansion. Some of this decline likely reflects decreased habitat-carrying capacity due to drought at the end of the Little Ice Age, but the unanticipated consequences of a European gift to North America were likely an even more important factor.

The appearance of the horse in North America during the 1600s, courtesy of early Spanish explorers, impacted Plains Indian culture as abruptly as the automobile changed our own three centuries later. Mounted and mobile, tribal hunters suddenly became highly efficient predators. For the first time, the horse also allowed them to hunt selectively, which unfortunately allowed the preferential harvest of bison cows, favored for their more tender meat. In addition to the horse's impact on Plains Indian hunting culture, feral horses (an estimated two million roamed the West by 1800) competed directly with bison for forage.

Despite a significant decline in numbers during the preceding two centuries, settlers headed West during the decades that followed the Lewis and Clark expedition certainly encountered staggering numbers of bison. In 1859 journalist Horace Greely described bison as follows during an extended western trip: "What strikes the stranger with the most amazement is their immense numbers. I know a million is a great many, but I am confident that we saw that number yesterday. Certainly, all we saw could not have stood on ten square miles of ground. Often, the country on either side seemed quite black with them. Consider that we have traversed more than one hundred miles since we first struck them, and that for the most of this distance the buffalo have been constantly in sight."

Similar descriptions appear in the notes of other well-known commentators ranging from Washington Irving to Wyatt Earp.

As late as 1870, George Bird Grinnell, heading west by train at the beginning of the Marsh expedition, reported a three-hour delay while one herd crossed the tracks. The development that nearly led to the extinction of the species occurred just two years later, when a young buffalo meat hunter named J. Wright Mooar shipped fifty-seven excess bison skins to his brother in New York, with instructions to test them on the British leather market. They proved a tremendous success, and a veritable gold rush in buffalo hides ensued.

Granted, bison had hardly been treated well during the preceding decades. Rail travelers shot them for amusement from moving trains and left the carcasses to rot, and the Union Pacific even organized expeditions dedicated solely to this purpose. Meat hunters—commercial and subsistence alike—slaughtered them just for their tongues. But nothing has ever motivated Americans to exploit wild resources as powerfully as money. By 1873, an estimated ten thousand professional hide hunters were operating on the plains.

The commercial hunters developed relentlessly efficient means of killing bison. Sharps rifles from Bridgeport, Connecticut, specifically designed for the commercial bison trade, delivered previously unheard of long-range accuracy and killing power. Commercial hunters learned to identify and pick off the natural leaders of the bison herds, allowing them to slaughter the dazed and confused remainder at their leisure. Organized outfits, including cooks, packers, and skinners, supported each rifleman; at 25 cents per hide, even a lowly skinner could earn as much in one day as an enlisted soldier made in a month. These developments all reflected the harsh realities of commercial market forces, which simply left no room for ethical considerations. As hide hunter Frank Mayer later observed in his memoirs, "I was a businessman. And I had to learn a businessman's way of harvesting the buffalo crop."

Harvest they did: Between 1872 and 1874, 850,000 hides left Dodge City alone. William "Buffalo Bill" Cody later recalled, "I killed buffalo for the railroad company for twelve months, and during that time the number I brought into camp was kept count of, and at the end of that period I had killed 4,280 buffalo." Even the commercial hunters realized that this kind of killing wasn't sustainable. As Mayer later noted, "It wasn't long after I got into the game that I realized the end of the buffalo was in sight." However, he concluded that prescient observation with a comment all too indicative of the market hunter's mentality: "I resolved to get my share."

With thousands of commercial hunters swarming the plains intent on "getting their share" by any means available, the great, free-ranging herds were obviously doomed absent immediate regulatory intervention. Even so, the speed of the bison population's collapse during the last three decades of the century proved shocking. Bison were eliminated from the central plains during the 1870s. The arrival of the Northern Pacific Railroad in Montana quickly led to the extermination of the remaining northern herd. In 1883, the railroad shipped 200,000 hides east from Miles City; by 1884, the number had fallen to 40,000. The following year, the haul fit inside a single boxcar, and that was the last hide shipment ever made from the area. By 1885, the newly published *History of Montana* (which was still four years away from statehood) declared the bison "almost an animal of the past."

As if the onslaught from commercial hunters wasn't enough to doom the bison herds, our military called for their deliberate destruction as a matter of policy that foreshadowed tactics the British would use against Afrikaners two decades later during the Boer War. Recognizing the dependence of the Plains Indians upon the bison, military strategists argued that eliminating the animals would effectively force the Indians into reservation confinement. "It is a sentimental error to legislate in favour of the bison," General Phil Sheridan wrote. "You should, on the contrary, congratulate the skin hunters and give each of them a bronze medal with on one side the image of a dead bison and on the other that of a distressed Indian. The hide hunters have done more to solve the Indian problem than the whole of the American Army in thirty years."

While some historians report that Sheridan invoked these views in testimony against a Texas legislative attempt to regulate the bison slaughter, others dispute whether this event actually took place. However, authorities agree that following the Battle of the Little Bighorn, army agents attempted to disrupt the bison herds' natural migration routes to and from Canada by burning grasslands along the border. The sole federal attempt to regulate the commercial bison harvest died of neglect on President Grant's desk because of Grant's belief in the theory that eliminating the bison would help subdue the Plains Indians and force them onto reservations.

Whatever Sheridan did or did not have to say about the subject in Texas, the prevailing attitude on the frontier certainly supported the notion that slaughtering bison and "civilizing" Indians went hand in hand. As lawman Wyatt Earp put it, "An examination of the record as a whole will show that the bad Indians were subdued into good Indians almost concurrently with the slaughter of the buffaloes, their one source of livelihood on the open range."

Policy makers who advocated starving the Indians into submission got their wish. By the end of the century, the Plains Indians were living destitute lives on reservations, and America's bison population had been reduced to a few survivors in Yellowstone National Park and in scattered private herds held together by individuals with the foresight to anticipate the species' near extermination.

Didn't anyone see the bison's fate coming? Indeed they did. George Catlin, the painter whose images introduced many Americans to the wilderness West, expressed his concerns as early as the 1830s: "It is a truly melancholy contemplation for the traveler in this country, to anticipate the period which is not far distant, when the last of these noble animals, at the hands of white and red men, will fall victims to their cruel and improvident rapacity." Writing in his diary in 1843 during his last journey west, John James Audubon observed: "Daily we see so many that we hardly notice them more than the cattle in the pastures about our homes. But this cannot last . . . before many years, the Buffalo, like the Great Auk, will have disappeared." (Ironically, James Bird Grinnell, who eventually led the fight to save the bison from extinction, read and commented upon these notes before he headed west on his first buffalo hunt in 1872.) Despite the eloquence of these concerns from observers of considerable public stature, the means to translate them into political action were not yet at hand.

History supports the thesis that it was commercial market hunting rather than sport hunting that destroyed the continent's bison population. But what about the "sportsmen" who killed hundreds of bison from railroad cars and left the carcasses for the scavengers? And the elaborate expeditions launched by sport hunters, most of them wealthy Europeans, that resulted in countless dead and abandoned bison during unregulated hunts for trophies and collections? Repugnant as those actions seem today, they probably had minimal effect on bison populations in comparison to the commercial harvest.

Bison continued to thrive across most of their range while populations of other game animals were being decimated east of the Mississippi simply because not many people could reach them. Prior to the intrusion of the railroad upon western habitat, European nobility were virtually the only parties with the time and money to mount expeditions into bison country. Even with the first railroads in place, commercial hunters were the only Americans motivated to pursue bison away from the tracks and into the heart of their remaining habitat. Furthermore, the hunters who engaged in those practices were not, by definition, sportsmen. While this distinction may seem a shallow semantic exercise, it stresses the importance of the developing code of ethics among American outdoorsmen. When these standards of conduct reached fruition in the twentieth century, they helped insure future generations of wildlife against precisely such abuses.

But they almost came too late to help the bison.

The American Shad

Because of the ease of harvesting them during their annual spring migration, shad played an especially important role in the early American food economy. When Jamestown Colony founder John Smith ventured up the Potomac in the spring of 1608, he found shad "lying so thick with their heads above the water, as for want of nets . . . we attempted to catch them with a frying pan, but we found it a bad instrument to catch fish with: neither better fish, more plenty, nor more variety for small fish had any of us ever seen in any place so swimming in the water."

Again, commercial harvest records bring some objectivity to these descriptions of abundance. George Washington himself operated a commercial shad fishery at Mount Vernon. In 1771 he caught 7,760 shad. After the Revolutionary War, several dozen commercial shad fisheries operated on the Susquehanna River; each took over 10,000 fish during the brief spring season. A single commercial operator took over 100,000 shad from his nets near what is now Brooklyn from 1790 to 1795.

Our first president himself nicely summarized the young nation's fish resources with this description of the Potomac near Mount Vernon: "This river . . . is well supplied with various kinds of fish at all seasons of the year, and in the spring with the greatest profusion of shad, herring, bass, carp, perch, sturgeon &c. Several valuable fisheries pertain to the estate; the whole shore, in short, is one entire fishery."

In the 1830s Dr. Samuel Howell operated a commercial shad fishery on the Delaware River near Philadelphia. Writing in 1837, he summarized prevailing attitudes toward the resource thus: "They [shad] afford a striking illustration of the goodness and design of an all-wise Providence, in making it a law of their nature that they shall thus annually throw themselves within the reach of man." The ability of early Americans to exploit their wildlife resources evidently benefited from confidence that God was on their side.

While shad populations never declined as precipitously or critically as the bison's, the abundance described in colonial records did not endure. The decline in shad returns to East Coast rivers between the Revolutionary War and the early 1900s was more prolonged and complicated than the collapse of the bison herds for several reasons. Because of the complexity of their life cycles, anadromous fish populations experience considerable natural fluctuations in number, and shad are no exception. Some of the rises and falls in shad numbers likely would have occurred independent of human activity. Furthermore, in contrast to the bison, shad faced more than one important proximate cause of their decline.

Again, intense commercial harvest pressure played its part. Shad remained the most important commercial food fish along the Atlantic coast throughout the nineteenth century. As late as the

1890s, the Delaware River produced between 10 and 20 million pounds of shad yearly for commercial nets. Chesapeake Bay turned out another 17 million pounds annually at the turn of the century. The total harvest along the Atlantic seaboard approached 50 million pounds per year. These huge figures not only attest to the vigor of the commercial fishery, but also demonstrate that the rapidly reproducing shad, in contrast to the bison, was able to withstand a century of intense harvest in remarkably sound condition.

But as with all anadromous fish, the true health of the shad population is measured not in global numbers, but by the watershed. A number of historically robust shad runs had suffered critical losses by the turn of the century as a direct result of human development along the coast.

Pennsylvania's Schuylkill River hosted tremendous shad returns during the colonial era, as reflected in the notes from William Penn cited earlier. Popular lore holds that the spring shad return to the Schuylkill saved Washington's troops from starvation after their bitter winter encampment at Valley Forge. While modern scholarship casts doubt upon that assumption (see John McPhee's *The Founding Fish*), the British took the possibility seriously enough to try (unsuccessfully) to divert the run downstream from Washington's camp.

American ingenuity and Manifest Destiny eventually succeeded where the Crown did not. Between 1813 and 1818, the Schuylkill Navigation Company constructed two dams on the upper river that kept returning fish from reaching much of their historical spawning ground. The construction of the Fairmont Dam in 1822 isolated returning shad from still greater reaches of the Schuylkill, and industrial pollution from gasworks in the lower river effectively ended the great historic runs.

Other rivers suffered similar fates, as noted earlier with regard to the Concord. In 1830 construction of dams on the upper Susquehanna began to deny returning shad access to their spawning waters there, although that river's once great runs were not completely destroyed until the completion of four large hydroelectric projects downstream in the early 1900s.

Since the definitive threat to shad populations derived from habitat destruction caused by human development and pollution as well as deliberate overharvest, it should come as no surprise that shad numbers declined most dramatically not in the nineteenth century, but the twentieth. By then, our ability to destroy the places wildlife lives had reached qualitatively new heights courtesy of the country's rapidly expanding economy and industrial base. The miracle, perhaps, is that the shad lasted long enough to face those new threats to their well-being—and benefit from the growing environmental awareness and sportsman-led initiatives that finally began to turn the tide in their favor.

At least some nineteenth-century Americans were prescient enough to see what lay ahead, even as commercial nets were harvesting millions of shad annually. In 1879 angler and pioneer fish culturist Seth Green wrote, "Shad are following in the wake of salmon in consequence of American energy of destruction." And as early as 1839, Henry David Thoreau, contemplating the inevitable impact of new commercial dams on the Concord, asked, "Poor shad! Where is thy redress?"

Their redress would have to wait until the following century, when America's sportsmen developed not just the conscience but the organizational resources needed to lead the fight that provided it.

EXTINCTION

No natural event defines ecological disaster like the death of a species. Death is forever, but when it happens to an individual, nature frankly doesn't care (the opinions of animal rights advocates notwithstanding). The genome is all that matters to the ecosystem, and, assuming successful propagation, the genes of the individual live on. The loss of a species is another matter entirely. When the last captive passenger pigeon died in 1914, countless years' worth of successful natural selection evaporated without a trace. Billions of pigeons had flown, fed, bred, and successfully reared their young for nothing. No thoughtful observer of natural history can fail to ask why.

When extinction befalls a game species, hunters provide a logical focus of blame, at least occasionally with some justification. Indeed, hunting is widely cited as the cause of the passenger pigeon's disappearance, often with an implicit warning that hunting threatens other game species with a similar fate. However, most biologists agree that extinction is seldom the result of a single event precipitated by human activity. (Exception: poorly adapted species that have evolved in highly isolated ecosystems like remote islands.) Let us examine the sad history of three game species— one well known, the other two relatively obscure—that became definitive casualties of nineteenth-century America's assault on wildlife and try our best to determine what role hunters really played in their demise.

The Case of the Missing Duck

John James Audubon's *Birds of America* includes portraits of several species no longer with us, including such well-known examples of things gone wrong as the Carolina parakeet and the ivory-billed woodpecker (which may or may not still haunt swamps in Arkansas). Today, however, few bird lovers weep for the first species to disappear permanently from the radar screen.

Plate #307 in *Birds of America* portrays—in the artist's distinctive, disembodied style—a pas de deux between a strikingly marked drake and disinterested hen identified as "pied ducks." Subsequent ornithological literature accords *Camptorhynchus labradorious* the common name "Labrador duck" in recognition of the species' presumptive breeding ground. Such taxonomic confusion is not remarkable, since a number of Audubon's birds are identified by names unfamiliar today. Contemporary records indicate that scoters and golden-eyes were also once called "pied ducks," so the term "Labrador duck" seems a reasonable way to avoid further confusion despite the lack of objective evidence that the birds ever spent time in Labrador.

Audubon's own notes acknowledge that he never encountered the species in the wild (his paintings were modeled on preserved specimens provided by friends). However, his portrayal matches contemporary descriptions of a scoter-size sea duck with—in the male—a dark body, white head, and black crown stripe and neck ring. The bird's most distinctive physical feature was the membranous enlargement at the base of the bill.

During the mid-1800s, the Labrador duck appeared in East Coast game markets during the winter months, where its table quality earned mixed reviews. No one really knows where it spent the summer breeding season; Labrador is probably as good a guess as any. The last reliable report of the bird in the wild came in 1875.

What killed off the Labrador duck? Overharvest by hunters remains a stock reply, but I have my doubts. The bird was at least a seasonal market species, but waterfowl that offered better table fare—and commanded accordingly higher market prices—survived additional decades of commercial hunting pressure before the advent of the modern conservation movement. Plume hunters also killed Labrador ducks for the millinery trade, but egrets and herons successfully endured far more intense harvest pressure for that market (albeit barely). Circumstances just don't register a convincing case for the prosecution against hunters—even market hunters.

No one knows exactly what made the Labrador duck disappear. This abrupt extinction-level event probably reflects some combination of market hunting pressure *and* a sudden habitat crisis (likely of human origin) *and* some tragic flaw locked deep within the vanished duck's genes. And who knows? Perhaps someday an astute coastal hunter will notice an odd black and white bird skimming the edge of his decoy spread, and the Labrador duck will be reborn just like the ivory-billed woodpecker.

The Last Heath Hen

On March 11, 1932, a farmer named James Green watched a barred, drably colored gallinaceous bird vanish into the brush on the island of Martha's Vineyard. *Vanish* is right—the bird was the last surviving heath hen in the world.

The ability to identify the exact date a species becomes extinct in the wild is highly unusual, but in this case the timeline was accurately documented. The species had disappeared from the East Coast mainland by 1870 at the latest, but the creation of the Heath Hen Reserve on Martha's Vineyard in 1908 allowed the island's remaining population to hang on tenuously for two more decades. The male to which Green said *adios* had been the lone survivor since 1928. When he disappeared into the bushes, so did the species.

For years, many biologists regarded the heath hen, *Tympanuchus cupido cupido,* as a subspecies of the midwestern prairie chicken, but recent DNA evidence suggests that it was probably a distinct species all along. Whatever its precise relationship to the prairie chicken, which it clearly resembled, the heath hen was certainly abundant along the eastern seaboard during the colonial era, as many eyewitness accounts attest. Since they were also easy to approach and kill, at least in comparison to other wild fowl staples like the turkey, they formed an important part of the colonial diet. (Some historians now suggest that the Pilgrims may have served heath hen rather than wild turkey at the first Thanksgiving dinner.) If roasted heath hen tasted anything like another close relative, the sharp-tailed grouse, it should have made fine dining. However, the birds were such an obligatory staple among the working classes in colonial America that servants actually negotiated with their employers to limit their heath hen dinners to two or three a week.

While subsistence hunting certainly accounted for a large share of the mainland heath hen population's decline, the fact that they were commonly fed to workers in large quantities also establishes the presence of a significant commercial market. Habitat alterations due to settlement and development certainly contributed to the species' demise, but commercial hunting was likely the principal factor.

As early as 1848, pioneering sportsman William Herbert (writing as Frank Forester) noted his outrage at both points:

> The destruction of the Pinnated Grouse [heath hen], which
> is total on Long Island and all but total in New Jersey and
> the Pennsylvania oak-barrens, is ascribable to the brutal
> and totally wanton havoc committed among them by the
> charcoal-burners who frequent those wooded districts; and
> who, not content with destroying the parent birds, at all
> seasons, even while hatching and hovering their broods;
> shooting the half-fledged cheepers in whole hatchings at a
> shot, and trapping them in deep snows—with a degree of
> wantoness equally barbarous, and unmeaning, steal or break
> all the eggs they can find. To this add the burning of the forest
> land, and you have more than enough to account for the
> extermination of the Pinnated Grouse.

The exact date of that extermination on the mainland remains unknown, but it had certainly occurred by 1870 at the latest, and possibly years earlier.

The remaining population on Martha's Vineyard provided Americans with an opportunity to attempt something they had never done before: take deliberate steps to save a species from extinction. Complete protection and the creation of the reserve allowed the island's population to grow to some two thousand birds within a few years. However, an epidemic of introduced avian blackhead disease and ferocious fires that destroyed vast amounts of habitat reduced that figure to unsustainable numbers. Despite the good intentions it represented, the reserve was not enough to save the heath hen from the effects of human activity: Blackhead disease likely arrived courtesy of domestic chickens, and fire suppression produced an abundance of understory fuel that led to the island's devastating wildfires.

What caused the final disappearance of the heath hen? Human activity is almost certainly to blame, and large-scale hunting for subsistence and the market were major contributing factors. However, the prairie chicken faced similar pressures and survived. (Although its range has been reduced considerably, greater prairie chicken numbers remain high enough today to allow regulated hunting in four midwestern states. The Attwater subspecies is listed as endangered, primarily due to habitat degradation by agriculture.) As in the case of the Labrador duck, other, undetermined environmental and genetic factors unique to the species likely doomed the heath hen the moment the first colonists stepped ashore at Jamestown.

The most important lesson from the heath hen may be that recognizing a species in crisis and acting vigorously to protect it does not ensure its survival if such efforts occur later than the tipping point at which a declining species reaches its minimal viable population, a concept of particular importance to slowly reproducing large mammals but ultimately applicable to all wildlife. Foresight is more important to the survival of species than desperation measures—a point American sportsmen eventually brought to the table with their twentieth-century emphasis on habitat conservation.

The Passenger Pigeon: An American Tragedy

Despite the inherent difficulty of making precise estimates of early colonial *Ecopistes migratorious* populations, contemporary accounts agree so unanimously that there can be no doubt about the passenger pigeon's original abundance. Descriptions of vast flocks appear in the notes of many early observers well known for other accomplishments. The explorer Samuel de Champlain reported "countless numbers" of pigeons in 1605, and Cotton Mather described a flock over a mile wide that required hours to pass overhead. America's first novelist, James Fenimore Cooper, included a similar description in *The Pioneers*. In 1673 John Josselyn wrote, "I have seen a flight of Pidgeons in the spring, and at Michaelmas, when they return back to the Southward, for four or five miles to my thinking had neither beginning nor ending, length or breadth, and so thick I could see no Sun."

In 1806 Alexander Wilson, the father of American ornithology and eponymous describer of the snipe and phalarope that bear his name today, described a flight one mile long and forty miles wide that he estimated contained over two billion birds. He also calculated the flight's daily nutritional needs as seventeen million bushels of food—a consideration that explains early American farmers' animosity toward the birds, even if it doesn't justify their willingness to slaughter them in defense of their crops.

Audubon provided countless valuable descriptions of early American birdlife above and beyond his paintings. He was not a flawless observer; for example, his mockingbird plate features a tree-climbing rattlesnake even though rattlers do no such thing, and a few of his species may never have existed. However, the remarkable overall accuracy of his bird portraits defines his credentials as a naturalist worth listening to, and he had plenty to say about the passenger pigeon. Describing events he observed near Louisville in 1813, Audubon wrote:

> The multitudes of Wild Pigeons in our woods are astonishing.
> Indeed, after having viewed them so often, and under so

many circumstances, I even now have to pause, and assure myself that what I am going to relate is fact. Yet I have seen it all, and that too in the company of persons who, like myself, were struck with amazement . . . I observed the pigeons flying from north-east to south-west, in greater numbers than I thought I had ever seen them before, and feeling an inclination to count the flocks, I dismounted, seated myself on an eminence, and began to mark with my pencil, making a dot for every flock that passed. In short time finding the task I had undertaken impractical, as the birds poured in countless multitudes, I rose, and counting the dots then put down, found that 163 had been made within twenty one minutes . . . The air was literally filled with Pigeons; the light of noonday was obscured as by an eclipse, the dung fell in spots not unlike the melting flakes of snow; and the continued buzz of wings had a tendency to lull my senses to repose.

John Muir devoted several pages of his autobiography to the passenger pigeon, including the following description: "I have seen flocks streaming south in the fall so large that they were flowing over from horizon to horizon in an almost continuous stream all day long, at a rate of forty to fifty miles an hour, like a mighty river in the sky, widening, contracting, descending like falls and cataracts."

While it's difficult to translate such descriptions into hard numbers, best modern estimates place North America's passenger population at three to five billion—*billion*, with a *b*—in the early 1800s. That's more than the continent's entire bird population today, and likely represented the largest aggregate of any vertebrate species at any time in world history. That abundance only makes the passenger pigeon's failure to survive the next century more remarkable.

While the lack of accurate records makes it hard to chart the decline in their numbers precisely, it seems likely that pigeon populations fell gradually from their all-time high between 1800 and 1850. While some contemporary observers noted fewer pigeons in anecdotal reports, this decline was not widely commented upon, and certainly wasn't obvious enough to arouse alarm (not that alarm ever did much for the passenger pigeon). Sport hunters certainly killed pigeons, but there weren't enough sport hunters in America—or enough lead shot—to have significant biological impact on a species numbering in the billions.

Hunting was certainly one primary cause of the precipitous drop in the pigeon population that took place during the 1870s and 1880s—but the responsible parties were market hunters, not sportsmen. Tastes in wild game as table fare fluctuate like hemlines on skirts. At the beginning of the nineteenth century, pigeon meat was largely regarded as a cheap source of protein fit for slaves and servants, but its popularity—and cash value—subsequently increased when railroads began to provide ready access to markets and the telegraph allowed market hunters to track migratory pigeon populations efficiently. The combination of new technology and increasing commercial demand is seldom beneficial to wildlife, but few species paid a price like the passenger pigeon.

The firearms used by American sport hunters in the nineteenth century really weren't efficient enough to threaten a bird population as large as the passenger pigeon's, but the techniques employed by market hunters were another matter. Unrestricted by law, conscience, and even the rudiments of a sporting ethic, they, like the buffalo hunters operating at the same time on the Great Plains, did what they needed to do to maximize their profits, and they did so with ruthless efficiency.

Highly gregarious birds, passenger pigeons congregated in huge nesting areas. One such roost site in Wisconsin covered 850 square miles and contained an estimated 136 million pigeons. Aided by increasingly modern means of communication and transportation, market hunters headed toward these high-density roost areas for the same reason Willy Sutton robbed banks: That's where the money was. With no concern for breeding seasons or bag limits, they set fire to nesting trees to drive flocks of pigeons into traps and nets. Captive, blinded birds became live decoys; set out on a stool to flutter, these decoys lured large flocks into the range of waiting nets and set guns (hence the origin of the term *stool pigeon*). Sulfur ignited beneath roost trees stunned birds and felled them to be picked up and killed by hand. Flightless squab were knocked from their perches with sticks. In Michigan, one flock sustained a take of fifty thousand birds per day for five months in 1878. A single commercial hunter shipped three million pigeons to market that year.

The birds' staggering original numbers allowed politicians a familiar means of dealing with their impending demise: They pretended that the problem did not exist. In 1857 the Ohio Senate considered a bill to protect the pigeon. A select committee convened to study the matter issued the following report: "The passenger pigeon needs no protection. Wonderfully prolific, having the vast forests of the North as its breeding grounds, traveling hundreds of miles in search of food, it is here to-day and elsewhere to-morrow, and no ordinary destruction can lessen them, or be missed from the myriads that are yearly produced."

By the time anyone realized that this apparently inexhaustible resource was anything but, it was too late. The Michigan legislature enacted the first statute banning the harvest of passenger pigeons in 1897, but there were no enforcement provisions and the pigeon population had suffered irreversible destruction by then anyway. By the time Americans recognized what was happening, the passenger pigeon was already doomed forever.

What killed this species? One way or another, we did; the disappearance of the passenger pigeon certainly resulted from human activities during the nineteenth century. However, the usual glib explanation—hunters shot them all—is more than a little simplistic. The birds had very precise habitat requirements: They needed large stands of mixed hardwoods as a source of both food (beechnuts, acorns, chestnuts) and shelter. Long before deliberate hunting of any kind began to impact their numbers, land clearing by farmers during the early phase of America's western expansion threatened critical pigeon habitat. Many of those same farmers viewed the vast flocks of pigeons much as ranchers viewed the wolves and cougars that preyed upon their livestock. A million pigeons could make short work of a grain field, and farmers slaughtered them during the early part of the century just to keep them out of their crops.

Nonetheless, hunters were certainly the proximate if not the sole cause of the species' disastrous decline during the late 1800s—but the term *hunter* comes with an important asterisk. The responsible parties were commercial market hunters, not sportsmen. Granted, the entire concept of a sporting ethic was in its infancy during the decades in which the passenger pigeon was reduced to oblivion. I am not excusing sport hunters from an active role in this debacle on the basis of altruism, but hunters who shot for enjoyment and the satisfaction of putting game on their own tables simply lacked the numbers, means, and resources needed to kill five billion pigeons, even if they'd wanted to.

The distinction between sport and commercial hunting is critical, and the decline and fall of the passenger pigeon illustrates it well. One way or another, the goal of the sport hunter is to have a good time. While that may sound appalling to some, it insulates the sport hunter from the practical need to kill, especially in large volume. The market hunter killed for different reasons. At the end of the day, nothing mattered more than the bottom line. In nineteenth-century America, market hunters recognized no impetus to conserve for the future and faced no legal or moral restrictions to their means of take. Take they did, and the passenger pigeon paid the ultimate price.

Habitat destruction, wanton slaughter, commercial greed . . . but while I'm certainly not eager to serve as an apologist for my own species' role in this miserable affair, I have to wonder if the passenger pigeon wasn't doomed the moment the first ax struck a tree at Jamestown. Some of our native species clearly had an innate ability to thrive in proximity to human settlement; the coyote and the white-tailed deer are two notable examples. Others did not, and the passenger pigeon was one of them. Like balls of baitfish in the sea, they depended upon their own sheer numbers and population density as defense against natural predators, an imperative that, in Darwinian terms, emphasizes the importance of survival of the species rather than the survival of individuals. Reached by any means, a certain minimum critical mass would have spelled the end, which is why last-ditch efforts to save the passenger pigeon by captive breeding were doomed to failure. Short of banning European settlement of the New World—an obvious impossibility—the passenger pigeon would have faced an uphill battle for survival under any circumstances.

The parallel example of the mourning dove supports this thesis. Smaller and far less numerous than the passenger pigeon, the second New World dove species early settlers encountered faced many of the same population pressures. Today, however, continental populations of the mourning dove are stable and likely at an all-time high of around 400 million, allowing an easily sustained hunting take of 30 million birds annually. One species worked; another, similar species didn't. While principles of natural law are consistent, they are not always fair.

I'm not giving nineteenth-century American sportsmen a free pass in the case of the passenger pigeon. If nothing else, too many of them stood by while catastrophes befell American wildlife, and even when they protested, the tone of those protests seems underwhelming by modern standards. But as difficult as it is to posit anything good coming from the total loss of species like the Labrador duck, heath hen, and passenger pigeon, I believe that something did. Shocked by what they had seen—even if, to take the most cynical point of view, for no reason other than enlightened self-interest—sportsmen began to articulate their concerns, and to organize. These early efforts went on to form the basis of the American conservation movement.

"Men still live," Aldo Leopold wrote in 1947, "who in their youth remember pigeons." Not any more. America's recognition of its responsibilities to its wildlife started too late for the passenger pigeon, the heath hen, and the Labrador duck, and, for our generation, the ability to remember them. But for a host of other species, it came just in the nick of time.

THE TIDE TURNS

In order to understand what American sportsmen started to accomplish in the field of wildlife conservation by the early 1900s, one must chart the change in attitude toward wildlife that began under their auspices a century earlier.

The interest in natural history shown by prominent citizens like Thomas Jefferson notwithstanding, the colonial American view of wildlife was almost strictly utilitarian. Fish and game were resources to be exploited according to need. Hunters and anglers killed and caught for food, predominantly for personal consumption, and for hides, as a source of leather for clothing and tools. In some cases, they eliminated large predators threatening livestock and, as in the case of the passenger pigeon, birds threatening crops.

While there is little evidence to suggest that the earliest colonists cared at all how, when, or what they killed, the limited scope of their needs and the simplicity and inefficiency of the tools available to them prevented them from having much impact on wildlife populations—for a while, at least. However, the prevailing view of fish, wild birds, and animals as part of an infinite resource that required no protection or regulation carried over far too easily into the heyday of nineteenth-century market hunting. From a population standpoint, wildlife really didn't need much protection from early frontiersmen armed with flintlocks and shooting venison for their families' immediate needs: Shot and powder were too scarce to squander, and the hunters were too busy staying alive to hunt or fish for personal enjoyment. But market economic forces, modern transportation, and increasingly efficient means of take eventually rendered that laissez-faire attitude obsolete.

The first Americans to articulate this realization were not conservationists, preservationists, ecologists, or wildlife lovers in any of the often confused and confusing modern meanings of those terms. No wonder—there weren't any in early nineteenth-century America. Rather, the first to question the unrestrained slaughter of wildlife were sportsmen rediscovering values derived from Europe, particularly the British Isles, where hunting and fishing had long been about more than putting meat on the table.

In England the notion that killing game and catching fish obligated the hunter or angler to some code of conduct dated back at least as far as Izaak Walton's seventeenth-century writings. Acceptance, largely voluntary, of restrictions on one's means and quantity of take in the field helped define the rigorous British class concept of the gentleman. Granted, in a time of dwindling European wildlife resources, gentlemen didn't rely on fish and game to feed their families, allowing them the luxury of a contemplative attitude toward wildlife impossible to imagine on the American frontier. But however undemocratic their origins, those ideas eventually formed the basis of standards critical to the preservation of wildlife in the New World.

Why did the concept of restraint in the field require two centuries to surface in America? The answer dates back to the first colonists, who found themselves facing formidable obstacles to everyday survival. The Pilgrims aboard the *Mayflower* came remarkably close to starving to death during their first year in the New World. Even by the time of the Revolution, settlers operating at the edge of the frontier lacked access to markets capable of supplying their routine food needs. Such circumstances simply didn't allow for ethical debates when an opportunity arose to kill a deer. Furthermore, American wildlife seemed inexhaustible, obviating any practical need to exercise restraint when killing it for personal use.

Finally, the idea of sporting ethics as practiced by gentlemen on the other side of the Atlantic no doubt evoked memories of the same class distinctions colonists had crossed the sea to escape. Contemporary wildlife law in England largely consisted of an elaborate series of statutes designed to reserve hunting rights for the landed and wealthy. The most onerous of these laws limited hunting privileges to citizens who owned specified amounts of land or enjoyed certain levels of income; others restricted the ability to own certain kinds of firearms to the same classes. The noted English jurist William Blackstone, who opposed these undemocratic "qualification" statutes on the basis of legal theory, lamented, "Fifty times as much property [is required] to enable a man to kill a partridge as to vote for a knight of the shire."

Faced with an abundance of game and virtually no legal hindrance to its taking, it's probably no wonder early colonial hunters ignored the constraints of "sportsmanship" as they had once known it on the other side of the Atlantic. When notions of ethics in the field finally resurfaced in America during the 1800s, they often did so courtesy of new arrivals from Europe, who faced an uphill battle to convince American outdoorsmen of their merits.

Consider this description of William Henry Herbert, a British aristocrat who immigrated to America in 1831, as written by a friend: "Like all true sportsmen, while fond of following game in season with gun, dog, and rod, he was a bitter and unrelenting enemy of all poachers and pot-hunters." From the wildlife standpoint, Herbert was clearly on to something. (In fact, writing under the name Frank Forester, he went on to become an important and articulate voice in the budding American conservation movement.) The trouble was that he had landed himself in a young nation populated by the same "poachers and pot-hunters" he despised.

The young country's growing prosperity during the half century between the Lewis and Clark expedition and the Civil War allowed at least some Americans the same kind of leisure time sporting gentlemen had enjoyed in Europe, and they began to occupy themselves in much the same way. These recreational hunters and anglers became the first to express concern for the future of America's wildlife resources, albeit motivated by a healthy measure of enlightened self-interest. Because of their personal familiarity with and affection for fish and game, they noted and protested its accelerating decline before any other element of our society. By the Civil War period, they were already longing for the good old days.

New York tackle dealer John Brown, author of the 1845 work *The American Angler's Guide,* lamented: "At your basse grounds, you take fewer and fewer fish, and [some] of your former places are now never visited by the sought for game. It is the commonest complaint of the old anglers that fishing nowadays is uncertain; that it is much more difficult to take a mess of fish; there are too many after them; in short, that 'times are not what they used to be,' and so also says the gunner of his favorite game."

Hunters and anglers have no doubt been whining about how much better things used to be since hunting scenes first appeared on cave walls at Lascaux. But as self-serving as such sentiments may be, sportsmen were virtually the only Americans to recognize the ongoing disappearance of wildlife and habitat, much less regret it.

After the Civil War, two developments arose that would have important implications for sportsmen and wildlife. The first was the appearance of magazines devoted to hunting and angling, beginning with the publication of *American Sportsman* in 1871. Prior to this event, there was no outdoor press as we know it today. While hunters and anglers had previously published descriptions of their activities in the field, these efforts were largely anecdotal and enjoyed limited public exposure at best. In contrast, *American Sportsman* was professionally produced, distributed nationally, and addressed topics related to hunting, angling, wildlife, and conservation in a single publication.

While *American Sportsman* was the first of its kind, the following decade saw the successful launch of several other outdoor magazines, including *Forest and Stream* (1873), *Field and Stream* (1874), and *American Angler* (1881). Had these publications limited their content to anecdotal "Me-and-Joe-went-hunting" fare, they wouldn't have mattered much to American wildlife. Fortunately, that was not the case. All consistently devoted considerable space to refining the concept of sporting ethics that had started to arise during the first half of the century. They also documented and protested the ongoing loss of wildlife and habitat at a time when such concerns received remarkably little attention from the mainstream press.

For the first time, American sportsmen enjoyed a forum that allowed them to articulate distinctions between meat and market hunters. In 1872 *American Sportsman* editor Wilbur Parker offered this definition of his periodical's title: "It is not about the mere killing of numbers, much less in the mere killing at all; it is not in the value of the things killed . . . It is not in the certainty of success—for certainty destroys the excitement, which is the soul of sport—but it is in the vigor, science, and manhood displayed—in the difficulties to be overcome . . . and above all in the *love of fair play*, that first thought of genuine sportsmen, that true sportsmanship exists."

While these lofty sentiments nearly sound trite today, and there is no way of knowing how many hunters and anglers actually adhered to them at the time, one must remember their context: For the previous two centuries, it had simply not occurred to Americans that they should scrutinize their conduct in the field or limit their bag and the means they employed to take it.

These early publications also expressed a consistent sense of dismay at America's vanishing wildlife that often ranged far beyond desire for more game to hunt and fish to catch. In 1875 Parker offered these thoughts on the country's approaching centennial:

> Shall we boast that where the deer, the buffalo, the salmon,
> and the feathered game . . . were once plentiful . . . we may
> now tramp for many a long summer day and not find a
> specimen? Shall we take credit for our predatory instinct that
> as individuals we have wasted natural gifts not exceeded in any
> other part of the world, and that as a nation we have been so
> intent upon multiplying the almighty dollar that we have given
> over our streams to pollution, our fish to destruction, and our
> land and water to the poacher and the exterminator . . . ?

This challenge would not seem out of place in a modern environmentalist newsletter. Its appearance in *American Sportsman* over a century ago is remarkable, and emphasizes how far ahead of their time sportsmen's concerns for wildlife and habitat really were.

In addition to the birth of an environmentally responsible American sporting press, the second key development during this time period was the rise of the sporting club. A few such organizations, located predominantly in the Northeast, sprang up during the early part of the nineteenth century, but their growth in number and influence became dramatic during the 1870s. *Forest and Stream* listed 308 such clubs in 1878, up from a third that number just four years earlier.

Many of these clubs formed simply to provide their members with places to hunt and fish. While they no doubt salvaged some important habitat in the process, those early contributions to the conservation movement had little overall implication for wildlife. Furthermore, dedicating private property to the exclusive outdoor recreational use of club members, most of them wealthy, evoked the old English qualification statutes and no doubt aroused considerable resentment from those on the outside looking in. Had the sporting club done nothing more than provide entertainment for its members, as wildly satirized in Tom McGuane's novel of the same name, American wildlife might have been better off without them.

Fortunately, self-interest and altruism merged nicely in the mission most of these organizations eventually defined. The majority made habitat preservation and wildlife protection a high—and in many cases, the highest—institutional priority. Growing rapidly in scope at the same time, the young sporting press provided a forum for these concerns and helped bring them to national attention. Writing about the club movement in an 1874 edition of *American Sportsman,* Parker noted, "The sportsmen of America are roused to the importance of banding themselves together for the purpose of checking and controlling the wanton waste and destruction of nature's best gifts intended for the heritage of universal man, and not for the benefit of the reckless and greedy few."

Records from the day suggest that these organizations were about substantially more than rich men escaping to the woods with whiskey and mistresses. *American Sportsman* documented the intentions of many such clubs, including reports such as these from 1873:

An association of gentlemen has been formed in Orange Co., NY, under the name of the Summit Lake Association for the purpose of propagating fish and game of various kinds.

At a meeting of the sportsmen in our town . . . a sportsmen's club was formed for the purpose of enforcing the game laws, the protection of game, and elevating the standard of . . . sportsmen, to be know as the Missouri Valley Sportsman Club.

Inspired rhetoric or hot air intended to make early sportsmen appear nobler than they really were? That's a legitimate question that defies a ready answer. There's no way to be certain how well sporting ethics translated from club minutes to the field. While these groups did lobby some legislatures, their political accomplishments were certainly modest at first, and their posture and tactics seem tame by the standards of environmental activism today. But again, the modern observer must place these efforts in their historical context. Even by the late 1800s, the concept that wildlife and its habitat deserved concerted intervention to salvage it for future generations was a radical idea that received virtually no attention from any other segment of American society.

Whatever their immediate effects upon conservation and the development of a sporting ethic, the rise of a strident outdoor press and organizations that allowed sportsmen to voice their concerns and marshal their resources for the benefit of wildlife deserve recognition for their historical importance. These developments provided an essential framework for crucial interventions by sportsmen on behalf of wildlife in the decades ahead, interventions about whose value there can be little doubt today.

GEORGE BIRD GRINNELL

D o times make the man, or vice versa? The question has been around as long as there have been historians to ask it. However, the remarkable reversal of fortune American wildlife experienced after its nearly complete destruction during the nineteenth century derived, at least initially, from the efforts of a few individuals whose vision anticipated the country's eventual, belated environmental awareness by several generations.

Virtually all were sportsmen before (and after) they became champions of wildlife conservation. Some, like Theodore Roosevelt, remain household names because of their accomplishments in other fields. Others, like Aldo Leopold, have become environmental icons in their own right, often celebrated by modern activists with no understanding of the role outdoor sport played in shaping their heroes' philosophy. Despite a remarkable record of accomplishment in the field—he probably did more to keep the American bison from going the way of the passenger pigeon than any other individual—George Bird Grinnell belongs to neither category. Compared to other giants in the field, his relative obscurity today seems unfortunate, if not downright shameful.

Born into a prosperous New York family in 1849, Grinnell enjoyed an American lineage that extended all the way back to the *Mayflower*. The seminal event of his childhood took place at age seven, when his father moved the family to the country. The Grinnells built a house in Audubon Park, a large unspoiled parcel of near-wilderness in what is now Manhattan. Although the celebrated painter had been dead for several years by then, the remainder of the Audubon family still inhabited the estate, including John James's elderly but dynamic widow, Lucy, and the Audubons' two grown sons, Gifford and Woodhouse, all of whom remained active in the family publishing business. Grinnell's relationship with the family was so strong that Lucy Audubon eventually willed him one of the few original Audubon paintings that she still retained.

This bucolic setting allowed Grinnell to indulge his fascination with natural history, aided and encouraged by direct tutelage from Lucy Audubon. He also learned to hunt there, often accompanied by the great painter's grandson Jack, who customarily carried his grandfather's rifle on their adventures.

Following a free-spirited but largely aimless adolescence, Grinnell headed to Yale in 1866. His academic career there remained largely undistinguished until 1870, when Professor Othneil Marsh, one of the preeminent natural scientists of the time, began to organize a major scientific expedition to what was then still America's wilderness West. Grinnell applied for and won a position on the team. The four-month expedition was a tremendous scientific success, resulting in the collection of fossils from over a hundred extinct species previously unknown to science. Young Grinnell's adventures, including encounters with wildlife, hostile Indians, and Buffalo Bill Cody, left him with well-developed outdoor skills and a sustained passion for the West.

Grinnell spent the next two years working as a stockbroker under the auspices of his father. He hated the work, and by 1872 had arranged to head west again, this time with the hope of participating in a traditional bison hunt with the Pawnee in northern Kansas. Grinnell accomplished his objective, and his later written descriptions of his hunting experiences with the Indians provide a fascinating record of a way of life that would not survive the decade.

Modern readers may be perplexed by the notion of the bison's future champion engaging in an organized buffalo hunt, even with Native Americans, at a time when the herds were beginning their precipitous descent. However, Grinnell was already drawing important distinctions. In an account of the hunt published later in *Forest and Stream,* he noted the care with which the Pawnees had salvaged every part of the dead bison for their use and contrasted their diligence with common practices elsewhere on the plains:

"How different would have been the course of a party of white hunters had they had the same opportunity. They would have killed as many animals, but would have left all but enough for one day's use to be devoured by the wolves or to rot upon the prairie."

Grinnell's next venture west took place in 1874, when he served as a naturalist accompanying Colonel George Armstrong Custer's expedition into the Black Hills of South Dakota. This expedition was less productive scientifically than Grinnell's first venture with Marsh; Grinnell apparently spent more time hunting for camp meat with his rifle than he did excavating fossils. But the expedition did lead to the discovery of gold in the Black Hills. The subsequent gold rush fractured the fragile peace with the Sioux, who held the Hills sacred, and set into motion events that eventually led to the Battle of the Little Bighorn.

After a brief stint back at Yale, where he served as a naturalist at the Peabody Museum, Grinnell went west once more in 1875, this time in the company of Colonel William Ludlow, a military engineer he had met during the Black Hills expedition. Their goal was to document the natural history of the recently created Yellowstone National Park, the nation's first. (While the creation of Yellowstone seems to defy the prevailing robber baron mentality that prevailing East Coast political and financial powers showed toward the West, the park likely received its initial federal approval because of strong support from the railroad lobby, which appreciated the revenue potential the development of the tourism industry might provide.)

In addition to Yellowstone's natural wonders, Grinnell experienced his first encounter with commercial hide hunters, who shared his fascination with the park's wildlife for different reasons. Although he himself had hunted game since childhood, Grinnell was appalled by what he saw, as noted in the introduction to his eventual report: "It may not be out of place here, to call your attention to the terrible destruction of large game, for the hides alone, which is going on in those portions of Montana and Wyoming through which we passed. Buffalo, elk, mule-deer, and antelope are being slaughtered by thousands each year, without regard to age or sex, and at all seasons. Of the vast majority of animals killed, the hide only is taken. Females of all these species are as eagerly pursued in the spring, when just about to bring forth their young, as at any other time."

Ludlow shared Grinnell's views about the need to protect the park and its wildlife from commercial exploitation, and both men issued strong statements to that effect upon their return. Grinnell's writings establish that he experienced an awakening of sorts during his time in Yellowstone. But in contrast to Audubon, Catlin, Thoreau, and others before him, he realized that eloquent protest would not be enough. Saving the West's wildlife would require vigorous political action, a novel concept among wildlife advocates at the time.

Back at Yale the following year, Grinnell received an interesting invitation from an old traveling companion. His decision to decline turned out to be one of the best things to happen to American wildlife during its period of extended trial, for the request was from George Armstrong Custer, who wanted Grinnell to accompany his Seventh Cavalry as a naturalist on an expedition up the Yellowstone River to the Bighorn Mountains. Had Grinnell accepted, he almost certainly would have become another casualty at the Battle of the Little Bighorn.

Instead of heading west to share in Custer's tragic folly, Grinnell spent 1876 editing a natural history column in *Forest and Stream*. Founder Charles Hallock immediately established an activist editorial tone remarkable for its day, chastising thoughtless hunters (at the time, it was accepted practice for upstanding citizens not just to flaunt the few existing game laws, but to brag about doing so), calling for wiser and more restrictive wildlife legislation, and emphasizing the need for its vigorous enforcement. Hallock even boldly challenged the government's odious if unofficial policy of subduing the Indians by destroying the last of the bison herds, hoping in print that "before many years, a just, honest, and efficient policy may be pursued toward the Indian, and that we can conscientiously aid in the increase in the buffalo instead of furthering its foolish and reckless slaughter."

While Hallock may have been way ahead of his time with regard to many issues facing wildlife and the developing West, he suffered a tragic flaw of his own: He drank too much. His ability to run the magazine faltered, and in 1880, at the age of thirty-one, Grinnell assumed both the editorship of the magazine and the presidency of its parent company.

Grinnell continued the magazine's aggressive policy toward despoilers of wildlife, and Yellowstone National Park became one of his first causes. Despite the park's alleged mandate as a haven for wildlife and a refuge from development, the pristine setting that Grinnell remembered from his 1875 expedition with Ludlow had come under relentless assault from the usual suspects, including freelance miners, commercial hunters, and development interests headed by the powerful railroad lobby.

The problem was simple to define. Despite lofty intentions at the time of its creation, the park fell outside the jurisdiction of any controlling legal authority as the territories of Montana and Wyoming and the federal government argued over the right to administer it—or not. Furthermore, the federal government had never authorized or funded any enforcement provisions for what few regulations were on the books. The resulting chaos created an open season for commercial hunters and developers. "The Park is overrun with skin hunters, who slaughter the game for their hides," Grinnell wrote, as he pointed out that Yellowstone "in thorough policing by good men, could be made a permanent breeding place for the larger wild animals which will otherwise, before long, become extinct."

None of those "larger wild animals" concerned Grinnell more than the bison. By the mid-1880s, Yellowstone was home to the only free-ranging bison herd left in America, and Grinnell was one of the few to recognize its importance. By 1890 their numbers were too low to support a trade in hides, but the same scarcity that should have created political pressure to save them produced another even more lucrative market: "trophy" heads for taxidermists who could sell them to collectors for $500 apiece, more than twice the annual salary of an enlisted cavalryman.

Although the congressional act that created the park directed the Secretary of the Interior to "provide against the wanton destruction of fish and game found within said park, and against their capture or destruction for the purchase of merchandise or profit," the lack of enforcement provisions and corruption of early park administrators like Robert Carpenter allowed commercial hunters to operate freely. One of the first concrete results of Grinnell's editorial lobbying was Carpenter's removal in 1885.

Another important event took place that year when Grinnell reviewed a book titled *Hunting Trips of a Ranchman* by a then little-known New York state assemblyman named Theodore Roosevelt. While lauding young Roosevelt's legislative work, Grinnell also questioned the depth of his experience in the West. Roosevelt objected to his characterization as a dude and visited Grinnell's office to state his case. Tempers soon cooled as the two men discovered their mutual interest in hunting and the preservation of wildlife. The friendship thus born eventually had major implications for the future of America's wild resources.

In addition to his longstanding concern for the preservation of large game animals, Grinnell recognized that birds of all sorts were facing the same pressure from commercial hunters as the bison. The passenger pigeon was disappearing, market hunters on the East Coast were slaughtering tremendous numbers of waterfowl with punt guns, and plume hunters were decimating populations of numerous species, particularly egrets and other wading birds, to feed the sudden demand for feathers in the fashion trade.

Writing in *Forest and Stream* in 1886, Grinnell proposed "the formation of an association for the protection of wild birds and their eggs, to be called the Audubon Society." The first national organization of its kind, the Audubon Society had fifty thousand members around the country by 1888. Today, the Audubon Society officially takes a neutral stand toward hunting, although its publications sometimes promote biologically unjustified anti-hunting points of view. It would behoove its modern members to recall that the Audubon Society's founder was very much a hunter—as, for that matter, was the remarkable naturalist and painter from whom the organization derives its name.

As far back as 1883, Grinnell had editorialized regularly against the ambitions of the rapacious Yellowstone Park Improvement Company, a private consortium that sought to maximize economic return from the park's resources. When the company began the construction of a large hotel near Mammoth, they cut corners on expenses by contracting with a commercial hunter to supply the labor force with twenty thousand pounds of meat from park wildlife. Pressure from Grinnell at *Forest and Stream* was largely responsible for Interior Secretary Henry Teller's eventual edict prohibiting the killing of all game within Yellowstone. Unfortunately, the new regulations again carried no provisions for enforcement.

With the editorial pages of *Forest and Stream* continuing to call attention to this deficiency in the defense of the park's wildlife, Yellowstone's lawlessness finally became too much to ignore. In 1886 Secretary of the Interior L. Q. C. Lamar dispatched Captain Moses Harris and fifty troopers from the First Cavalry to the park to enforce the law. Harris took his job seriously and preformed it dutifully, apprehending and expelling large numbers of poachers. Unfortunately, there were no legal means to enforce their incarceration, so all he could do to those who returned was expel them again. Furthermore, even fifty competent troopers couldn't adequately patrol an area the size of Yellowstone. Despite the first serious attempt at fish and game law enforcement the park had ever seen, commercial poachers continued to operate.

Meanwhile, Yellowstone National Park as a whole faced even sterner challenges from the ever-relentless railroad lobby, which eagerly sought a development corridor through critical winter game habitat along the northern edge of the park. Unfortunately for development interests, Grinnell and his supporters, including Roosevelt, had learned a lot about lobbying themselves over the course of the previous decade. Grinnell entered the latest fray using his customary tactics: a bruising series of *Forest and Stream* editorials highlighting the threat to wildlife and Yellowstone's future posed by the railroad's attempt to secure a huge swath of land within the park by congressional grant.

He and Roosevelt then engaged in some direct political lobbying of their own. After convincing the four-year-old Boone and Crockett Club to adopt a resolution opposing any railroad operations in the park, influential club members personally buttonholed key cabinet officials and legislators and expressed their opposition to the rail lobby's proposal.

Finally, Grinnell turned to mass appeal, encouraging all *Forest and Stream* readers to flood their representatives' offices with pamphlets, including Grinnell's editorials and a letter from Roosevelt, by then a federal Civil Service commissioner, urging "all public spirited Americans to join with *Forest and Stream* in the effort to prevent the greed of speculators careless of everything save their own selfish interests, from doing the damage they threaten to the whole people of the United States."

In an America that still largely viewed its wild resources as a basis for economic exploitation and little else, this call to arms was remarkable. Indeed, the congressional debate over the railroad's proposal produced abundant examples of the prevailing political sentiment. Senator James Berry of Arkansas made a suggestion to "sell it [Yellowstone] to the highest bidder and place the money in the Treasury" (shades of the recent, notorious, and thankfully failed Pombo Amendment). And there was this from Representative Joseph Toole of Montana: "The right and privileges of citizenship, the vast accumulation of property, and the demands of commerce" should not "yield to the caprice of a few sportsmen bent only on the protection of a few buffalo in the National Park." It's depressing to realize how contemporary that screed sounds relative to environmental issues today, although no doubt modern development interests would express their aims a bit more subtly . . . perhaps accompanied by images of bucolic bison grazing beside a railroad track.

Despite these efforts from sportsmen's groups, a bill authorizing the sale of park territory to the Northern Pacific Railroad passed the Senate and appeared destined to become law. Then Grinnell somehow obtained a copy of a telegram from a Washington lobbyist to the governor of Montana urging political pressure on House Speaker Charles Crisp to secure a suspension vote on the bill—a routine if underhanded legislative tactic. Grinnell brought his full muckraking tactics to bear upon the matter, publishing the telegram in *Forest and Stream* and accusing Crisp of collusion with the railroad lobby. Deciding that a major political scandal was more threatening than the wrath of the railroad industry, Crisp let Congress adjourn without bringing the bill to the floor. This was probably the closest political call Yellowstone Park and its wildlife ever experienced.

When Grinnell and his cohorts successfully lobbied against new bills to cede Yellowstone land to the railroad in the next session of Congress, victory in the political battle over the park's integrity seemed secure. But law enforcement in Yellowstone was another matter. The park and its wildlife received a boost with the appointment of Captain George Anderson to the superintendent's position in 1893. Like Harris before him, he proved capable and aggressive, but still lacked the resources to rid Yellowstone completely of poachers like the notorious Edgar Howell, who made regular forays from Cooke City into the buffalo wintering grounds in the northeast corner of the park, where he tracked the animals on crude skis until they foundered in the deep snow, allowing him to dispatch them and salvage the capes and heads for the taxidermy market.

In March 1894 Anderson's dedicated scouts apprehended Howell with five freshly killed bison in a daring backcountry law enforcement raid. By coincidence, Grinnell had dispatched *Forest and Stream* reporter Emerson Hough to Yellowstone that winter to report on the status of the park's wildlife, and Hough was at Mammoth when Anderson received word of Howell's capture. Hough provided firsthand reporting of the incident, supplemented by photographs shot by F. Jay Haynes. Grinnell published these reports and circulated them widely, emphasizing an ultimate irony: Under existing law, the only punishment Howell faced was confiscation of his booty and expulsion from the park.

Widespread public outrage, especially from fellow sportsmen, allowed Grinnell and other Boone and Crockett Club members, including Roosevelt and Iowa congressman John Lacey, to lobby effectively for legislative redress. With remarkable speed—particularly in light of the previous decade's sad failure to provide protection for the park—the Lacey Act of 1894 (not to be confused with Lacey's more widely known bill of 1900) passed both houses of Congress and was signed into law by president Grover Cleveland, an ardent sportsman himself. In addition to reaffirming the previous prohibition against killing park wildlife, the bill provided meaningful penalties for its violation (up to $1,000 in fines and two years in jail), as well as specific funding for law enforcement. Congress soon extended the bill's provisions to include other national parks, and it remains a foundation of federal wildlife law today.

By 1902 the park's bison herd was down to twenty-three animals. Beyond doubt, subsequent efforts to save the species would have come too late except for Grinnell's early, relentless appeals to the public conscience.

While the passage of the first Lacey Act finally allowed Grinnell some relief from his concerns about Yellowstone and its wildlife, he was not one to rest on his laurels. In addition to remaining editor of *Forest and Stream* for thirty-five years, he became a highly regarded Native American ethnologist and devoted most of his eventual twenty-nine books to recording their vanishing way of life, becoming an honorary member of the Blackfoot tribe in the process. He spent years exploring the remote territory in what is now Glacier National Park, and was instrumental in the park's creation by President William Taft in 1910.

Today, of course, no hunting is allowed in Yellowstone. Nonetheless, Grinnell's early, spirited defense of the park remains highly relevant to modern sportsmen, and to the thesis of this book. The creation of Yellowstone Park represented the country's first large-scale attempt to preserve a portion of its wildlife and protect it from the relentless force of economic development; as such, it became the prototype for countless similar battles still being waged today.

Grinnell convincingly demonstrated the power of a responsible outdoor press in the fight to preserve wildlife and habitat. His key role in the founding of the Audubon Society and the Boone and Crockett Club established important models for the numerous wildlife advocacy organizations that would arise in the twentieth century. Finally, he demonstrated that sportsmen could and would not just accept but champion appropriate restrictions on hunting when the common good called for it, as it did in the case of Yellowstone's wildlife. One can only wish that non-hunting wildlife advocates might be as willing to compromise today.

Grinnell died in New York in 1938 at the age of eighty-eight, hailed by the press as "the father of American conservation." The title might just as well have read "the father of American sportsmanship." Grinnell's regard for the wild began when he hunted Audubon Park as a boy, and he never renounced his love of the chase. Instead, he redefined its terms to include the need for discipline and restraint in the field, regard for wildlife as valuable for reasons beyond simple economics, and the moral obligation to care for the places wildlife calls home.

THE BOONE AND CROCKETT CLUB

The first American sportsmen's clubs were small and largely social, originally serving few ambitions beyond companionship in the field and the opportunity to share stories (some possibly true, many accompanied by food and drink with particular emphasis on the latter). The 1870s brought both an explosion in the number of such clubs (most in the East, some in the South, and few in the West) and a shift in their purpose.

The clubs' increase in number and change in mission arose for two reasons. The first was the decreasing availability of land available for hunters and anglers to engage in their favorite sports, a consideration that helps explain the geographic concentration of these clubs in the increasingly crowded East. Many of the new clubs used group purchasing power to acquire property suitable for hunting and fishing, just to give their members secure opportunities to participate in outdoor sports. The second, and originally less significant, factor was growing concern for the future of American wildlife, spurred on by an increasingly confrontational outdoor press.

Unfortunately, despite frequent good intentions, the early clubs didn't accomplish much on behalf of wildlife except provide occasional islands of habitat secure from development. The clubs were small and politically unsophisticated. Their members were often more interested in going fishing than engaging in the drudgework effective political activism requires (a trait shared by many sportsmen today). When they did tackle wildlife and conservation matters, the issues were usually local. The concept of a sportsmen's organization as an effective force in national wildlife politics had to wait until 1887 for its realization. And to think that it all began with a confrontation between a cocky young outdoor writer and an editor!

While the friendship that developed between George Bird Grinnell and Theodore Roosevelt eventually had tremendous implications for wildlife, it got off to a rocky start, as noted earlier. Young Grinnell's 1885 review of Roosevelt's first hunting book, *Hunting Trips of a Ranchman,* showed little evidence of the tact and diplomacy that would eventually serve him and his cause so well. In addition to questioning Roosevelt's credentials as an experienced western outdoorsman, he went on rather unnecessarily to suggest that a cow elk in one of the book's illustrations looked like a "hydrocephalus dwarf." Fortunately, Roosevelt was forthright enough to take his concerns directly to Grinnell and listen to what he had to say, and Grinnell was sufficiently conciliatory to appease Roosevelt once he recognized a potentially valuable ally in his battle on behalf of conservation. The truce the two established during their meeting in the *Forest and Stream* office following the publication of Grinnell's review produced countless benefits for conservation, none more tangible than the founding of the Boone and Crockett Club two years later.

The two needed little time to establish common ground. "We talked of [the commercialization of wildlife] at length," Grinnell recalled years later in his introduction to Roosevelt's collected works, "and in a vague way foresaw the dangers that already threatened big game in many parts of the West as soon as a point should be reached where their products could be turned into dollars."

Grinnell was already thinking about the need for a strong national organization to represent sportsmen's interest in wildlife conservation, as noted in an 1884 *Forest and Stream* editorial in which he called for an "association of men bound together by their interest in game and fish, to take active charge of all matters pertaining to the enactment and carrying out of the laws on the subject." The Audubon Society he founded in 1886 limited its scope to the preservation of birds, but getting the society off the ground taught Grinnell important lessons about what it took to start a national conservation organization. In December 1887 Roosevelt hosted a dinner party to launch a new group dedicated to the hunting and conservation of big game animals. In addition to Grinnell, the guest list included a number of wealthy, prominent New York citizens best described in modern terms as heavy hitters.

The club's founders identified five objectives at the outset:

(1) To promote manly sport with the rifle. (2) To promote travel and exploration in the wild and unknown, or but partially known, portions of the country. (3) To work for the preservation of the large game of this country, and, so far as is possible, to further legislation for that purpose, and to assist in enforcing the existing laws. (4) To promote inquiry into, and promote observations on the habits and natural history of, the various wild animals. (5) To bring about among the members the interchange of opinions and ideas on hunting, travel, and exploration; on the various kinds of hunting rifles; on the haunts of game animals, etc.

Some, like the first, sound dated (quaintly or otherwise, depending on one's gender). Others, such as the third, seem quite modern. Considering the tone of both men's later writings, it's hard not to hear Roosevelt's voice in the former, with Grinnell's deferred to in the latter. But then, it was Roosevelt's dinner party.

The club's original rules restricted membership to one hundred individuals (all male according to edict, all well-off Caucasians according to the social stratification of the times), each of whom had to "have killed with the rifle in fair chase, by still-hunting or otherwise, at least one individual of three of the various kinds of American large game." Although the record remains unclear, it was likely Grinnell who argued successfully for the eventual inclusion of important non-hunting conservationists like geologist Arnold Hague and attorney William Phillips, who, as congressmen, aided Grinnell in his defense of Yellowstone. The club amended its rules to allow non-hunters like Hague and Phillips (an avid angler) to become associate or honorary members—an example of inclusivity that both sides of the hunting versus non-hunting divide in the modern conservation movement would do well to emulate.

One of the club's first accomplishments was to affirm budding standards of outdoor ethics and fair chase—principles governing what sportsmen should and should not do in the field even when no law addressed the subject. The club's original constitution specifically forbade "killing bear, wolf or cougar in traps," "killing game from a boat while it is swimming in water," "fire-hunting" (what we'd call jacklighting today), and "crusting" (killing animals immobilized in deep snow, a favorite tactic of market hunters operating in Yellowstone National Park). The Alaska Native "subsistence" practice of running down swimming caribou in motorboats and dispatching them with modern firearms aside, most of these proscriptions seem obvious today. At the time, however, their official codification by an organization of individuals as prominent as the club's members represented a dramatic advance in the evolution of the sportsmen's concept of voluntary self-restraint.

The club's leaders chose local issues in their earliest attempts to influence policy, and since the majority of the original members were New Yorkers, the Adirondacks predictably became the venue for their first tangible success. The immediate issue was deer "hounding"—using dogs to drive deer into lakes, where they were easily shot or clubbed to death. Grinnell had long editorialized against the practice, and after he organized a petition drive to make it illegal, the New York legislature outlawed hounding in 1885. However, protests from moneyed interests including lodge owners, guides, and wealthy downstate "sportsmen" (remember that the concept of sportsmanship was very much a work in progress) resulted in the prohibition's repeal the following year. Club president Theodore Roosevelt initiated an intensive lobbying campaign by influential club members, and New York eventually passed a law prohibiting both hounding and jacklighting, legislation that quickly became a model for similar laws in other states.

Yellowstone's ongoing wildlife crisis provided an opportunity for the Boone and Crockett Club and its well-connected members to exert a positive influence for wildlife at the national level. In 1890 development interests' attempts to push a railroad through the park's northern reaches represented an immediate threat. Roosevelt actually waffled on the issue at first, but once Grinnell convinced him that such a rail corridor would be a disaster, he went to work in defense of the park's integrity. At the club's annual banquet in 1891, he loaded the guest list with influential Washington insiders, including the Secretaries of War and the Interior, the Speaker of the House, and a half dozen other congressmen, who then heard him read the club's position statement on Yellowstone:

> Resolved, that the Boone and Crockett Club, speaking for
> itself and hundreds of clubs and associations throughout
> the country, urges the immediate passage by the House of
> Representatives of the Senate bill for the protection and
> maintenance of Yellowstone National Park. Resolved, that
> this club declares itself unanimously opposed to the granting
> of a right of way to the Montana Mineral Railroad or to any
> other railroad through the Yellowstone National Park.

A lively discussion followed, a number of the politicians present expressed real interest in the park's wildlife, and Grinnell and Roosevelt left feeling optimistic. While the railroad lobby did succeed in blocking the reform measure in the House, the Boone and Crockett Club had not yet begun to fight.

Grinnell's relentless editorializing in favor of keeping Yellowstone free of commercial development eventually spurred the mainstream press to adopt similar positions. When asked to head a "Defense Association" to lobby on behalf of Yellowstone, Grinnell deferred to the Boone and Crockett Club, which had finally expanded its membership base for the sake of increased political clout. Roosevelt and other influential club members testified in favor of protection for the park at hearings by the House Public Lands Committee. Their lobbying resulted in the passage of the Lacey Act of 1894.

The club's political activism eventually helped wildlife far beyond Yellowstone's borders. In his 1910 book *A Brief History of the Boone and Crockett Club,* Grinnell posited that "the attempt to exploit Yellowstone National Park for private gain in a way led up to the United States forest reserve system as it stands today" (i.e., the USDA Forest Service).

In fact, the Boone and Crockett Club had been lobbying for some form of rational forest management for years before passage of the first Lacey Act. Supreme Court attorney Phillips, an associate member of the club thanks to the farsighted change in its initially restrictive membership rules, played an especially important role as an advocate and lobbyist for the nation's woodlands. As Grinnell later recalled in his club history, Phillips "succeeded in interesting Mr. Lamar, Secretary of the Interior, and a number of Congressmen, in the forests, and all of those persons began to work together." There is no doubt that the Boone and Crockett Club played a significant role in the eventual creation of the Forest Service.

The club's attempts to define standards of sportsmanship and fair chase may have been as important to wildlife as its early political activities. Americans who hunted—for subsistence and recreation alike—had instinctively bridled against government attempts to regulate their activities in the field ever since the colonial era. In the days of apparently unlimited wildlife resources, they saw no rationale for such restrictions, which evoked memories of the same class-based limitations on hunting they had escaped from in the British Isles. "Hunting was the labor of savages in North America, but the amusement of gentlemen in England," Samuel Johnson observed, as reported by James Boswell. The problem for wildlife was that democratic Americans for the most part had no interest in the inconvenience of rules—written and otherwise— that only the wealthy could afford to apply to the pursuit of game in England. Hounding and jacklighting were just the kind of activities the British gentry banned in order to ensure a monopoly upon game for themselves.

Self-regulation—the imposition of rules by sportsmen upon themselves and other sportsmen—represented a qualitative departure from the highly codified system of restrictive laws (and heavy penalties) that would-be hunters and anglers of ordinary means had known in Europe. (Poaching was one of a number of minor crimes that could result in forced "transportation" from England to Australia.) Attempts to articulate such standards of conduct began in America during the early nineteenth century, but the Boone and Crockett Club's constitutional prohibition against certain widely accepted hunting practices represented the first major attempt to formalize them. Granted, the upper-class background of virtually all of the club's early members made these self-imposed restrictions echo Old World class distinctions and no doubt aroused resentment among outdoorsmen of lesser means and different social standing. But they also formed the legitimate basis for a necessary, restrictive code of conduct that would eventually be refined further by sportsmen like Roosevelt and Aldo Leopold, and become the foundation for many important elements of modern wildlife regulations.

As former Interior Secretary Stuart Udall observed later, "When Theodore Roosevelt became President, the Boone and Crockett wildlife creed . . . became national policy." Whatever objections one might raise to some of the dated attitudes expressed in the early history of the Boone and Crockett Club, it would be difficult to name a modern president who has entered office with a better basis for national policy toward wildlife.

As most modern sportsmen know, the Boone and Crockett Club remains alive and well today. The club is perhaps best known for its *Records of North American Big Game*. Known among riflemen simply as "the Book," these records tabulate and rank the continent's big game trophies according to the club's own standardized measurement system, which has been copied by several other record-keeping organizations including the Pope and Young Club, Boone and Crockett's archery counterpart. However, record-keeping functions only account for some 10 percent of the club's annual budget, the remainder of which is earmarked for conservation and wildlife education purposes.

In 2000 the club played an instrumental role in the creation of American Wildlife Conservation Partners, an umbrella organization dedicated to providing sportsmen of various backgrounds with a unified lobbying voice on Capitol Hill. Boone and Crockett recently negotiated the purchase of Theodore Roosevelt's historic 23,000-acre Elk Horn Ranch in North Dakota, converting it from a private cattle ranch to public property managed for wildlife and administered by the Forest Service. And in a visionary educational project, the club recently endowed a Professorship in Wildlife Conservation at the University of Montana. That program has trained two dozen fellows from around the country and is currently being duplicated at Texas A&M, Michigan State, and Colorado State universities.

The modern Boone and Crockett Club deliberately places less emphasis on "the Book" that made it famous and more on the core conservation values championed by its founders. No matter how one feels about record books, every wildlife advocate owes the Boone and Crocket Club a historic debt whether they enjoy the outdoors while carrying a rifle, bow, camera, or binoculars, or simply appreciate the satisfaction of knowing that wildlife is alive and well in North America.

BULLY PULPITS AND BIG STICKS:
THE ROOSEVELT ADMINISTRATION

Whether the subject is athletes or politicians, historical rankings are as irresistible as they are subjective, none more so than attempts to determine our best and worst presidents and how any one stacks up against all the rest. One recent summary examined twelve such rankings compiled by professional historians between 1948 and the present, reflecting the opinions of over a thousand academics and journalists who study American history professionally. Only five presidents received a ranking of seventh best or higher in all twelve polls: Washington, Jefferson, Lincoln, and the two Roosevelts, Franklin and Theodore. The latter must have been a remarkable individual indeed to have done so much for wildlife while he was busy leading the country so well.

Reducing a life like Roosevelt's to a book chapter may seem presumptuous, but it's impossible to appreciate the contributions he made to conservation as president without appreciating the man behind them. Roosevelt was born in 1858 to a wealthy, civic-minded New York family (his father helped found both the Metropolitan Museum of Art and the American Museum of Natural History). Debilitating illness (severe asthma), nearsightedness, disciplined enthusiasm for athletics, and intense fascination with natural history characterized his childhood. At age eighteen he entered Harvard, where a distinguished academic record almost led him into a career as a professional naturalist. During college breaks he spent as much time in the outdoors as possible, and he killed his first deer on a trip to Maine in 1879.

After graduating with honors, he gravitated to politics instead of biology, and in 1881 became the youngest representative ever elected to the New York State Assembly. "I am fond of politics," he confided to a friend at the end of his first term, "but fonder still of big game hunting." With his youthful priorities thus in order, he made his first trip west in 1883, during which he killed a buffalo and purchased a cattle ranch in the Dakota Territory.

During his three terms in the New York legislature, Roosevelt pursued an aggressive reformist agenda that endeared him to the popular press, if not to his Republican Party's reigning elders. Although not yet a crusading conservation activist, he did back measures protecting the Adirondacks from irresponsible development and commercial hunting.

In 1884 tragedy struck when his wife, Alice, and his mother both died unexpectedly on the same day. Depressed and disillusioned with politics after the nasty Republican convention two months later, Roosevelt again headed west, where he began work on *Hunting Trips of a Ranchman* and ran his ranch until the devastating blizzard of 1887 destroyed most of the livestock on the Great Plains, including his.

After returning from the West, Roosevelt married his second wife, Edith; lost a mayoral campaign in New York City; wrote industriously; and helped George Grinnell found the Boone and Crockett Club. By 1889 he was serving in Washington as a public service commissioner and acquiring a reputation as an outspoken political maverick. In 1895 he accepted appointment as commissioner of New York's notoriously corrupt police department and attracted growing attention as a reformer.

In 1897 President William McKinley appointed him Assistant Secretary of the Navy. Again, Roosevelt affected policy and attracted headlines out of all proportion to the importance of the post. He lobbied publicly for war against Spain after the sinking of the *Maine* in Havana harbor, and when Congress declared war in 1898, he resigned his post and began assembling a volunteer cavalry unit. By the time the brief war ended a few months later, Roosevelt had led his Rough Riders up San Juan Hill (in an action most military historians praise more for its bravado than its tactical judgment) and become a national hero.

His new popularity helped him win election as New York's gov-ernor in the fall of 1898. In addition to pursuing economic reforms and improved working conditions for laborers, Roosevelt formulated a plan to protect the state's forest preserves, aided by his new friend Gifford Pinchot, who would soon head the agency that became the Forest Service. Threatened by his activism, Republican Party bigwigs decided Roosevelt would be less trouble in Washington. In what must have seemed like a brilliant idea at the time, they conspired to nominate him as McKinley's vice-presidential running mate in 1900. After helping McKinley win the election, Roosevelt might have languished in the vice-presidential political graveyard, but when the anarchist Leon Czolgosz assassinated McKinley the following year, American wildlife suddenly acquired the ultimate friend in high places.

Roosevelt's subsequent eight years in the White House (a term he himself coined for what was previously known as the Executive Mansion) produced far too many political accomplishments out-side the field of conservation to catalog here, but his work on behalf of wildlife and wild places alone would have guaranteed him high historical regard. For the first time in American history, a president assumed office with wildlife his highest priority, not the lowest. "Conservation of natural resources is the fundamental problem," he declared from the start. "Unless we solve that prob-lem, it will avail little to solve all others." One of his first acts after leaving McKinley's funeral was a meeting with Pinchot to begin planning a national conservation policy.

One of Roosevelt's first concrete federal legislative accom-plishments was the 1902 passage of the National Reclamation Act (over the staunch opposition of many western legislators, a pat-tern that persisted throughout his presidency). The bill authorized and funded a cadre of civil engineers under the auspices of the National Geological Survey with the goal of constructing a vast series of dams to "conserve" water throughout the arid regions of the West. By contemporary standards, that sounds more like a problem than a solution. One can only appreciate its significance within the context of the time.

At the beginning of the twentieth century, some 560 million acres of federally owned land lay scattered about the West, most of it devoid of any controlling legal authority. Legislative leftovers from the Manifest Destiny era, such as the 1866 Mineral Land Act, the 1873 Timber Culture Act, and the 1877 Desert Land Act, allowed multiple avenues for development with virtually no resources allocated for management or regulation, however necessary. As railroads closed the gap between these remote lands and markets for the resources they contained, a corrupt system of exploitation began to thrive. Many of the early parties who filed 160-acre land claims under the Homestead Act, for example, promptly signed their titles over to organized conglomerates interested in timber, minerals, and unrestricted grazing rather than breaking sod.

Roosevelt recognized the threat to wildlife and habitat these schemes posed and entered office determined to bring them to a halt. While the Reclamation Act would hardly sound like sophisticated legislation to a modern conservationist, it was the beginning of the federal government's effort to control and manage remote lands it owned on behalf of the public. Environmental icon John Muir recognized the importance of such principles when he wrote: "God has cared for these trees, saved them from drought, disease, avalanches, and a thousand straining, leveling tempests and floods; but he cannot save them from fools. Only Uncle Sam can do that."

At the time, what minimal management these federally owned properties received was both fragmented (among the Land Office within the Department of the Interior, the Geological Survey, and the Department of Agriculture's Division of Forestry) and inept. "The forests were run by clerks," Roosevelt wrote later, "few if any of whom had ever seen or set foot on the timberlands for which they were responsible." Roosevelt quickly addressed these shortcomings by consolidating all management within the Department of Agriculture's Division of Forestry and granting broad authority to its new supervisor, Gifford Pinchot, his personal friend and a professionally trained forester.

Modern-day activists make much of the supposedly iron-clad distinction between "conservationists" and "preservationists." However valid that dichotomy today, its roots can be traced directly back to Roosevelt's administration in the persons of two individuals: Pinchot and Muir. Nearly alone among the personalities profiled in this book, neither was a sportsman. (Pinchot fished some in his youth and didn't seem to care about hunting one way or the other. Muir was openly skeptical about hunters.) Roosevelt considered both men friends nonetheless, and even Muir expressed high regard for Roosevelt in his writing. Pinchot worked closely with the president throughout his administration as they laid the groundwork for what would eventually become the Forest Service. When Roosevelt needed respite from the political hurly-burly in 1903, he retreated to the wilds of Yosemite with Muir. Both men clearly influenced him politically and philosophically.

Pinchot represented the archetypical "conservationist." In fact, he claimed credit for coining the term during his tenure as the Roosevelt administration's chief forester (even though George Grinnell had used it decades earlier in *Forest and Stream*). While his own writings establish his esteem for woodlands and the political record confirms how hard he was willing to fight for their proper management, his concerns were ultimately and consistently utilitarian: "The first great fact about conservation is that it stands for development. There has been a fundamental misunderstanding that conservation means nothing more than husbanding resources for future generations. There could be no more serious mistake. Conservation does mean provision for the future, but it means also and first of all the recognition of the right of the present generation to the fullest necessary use of all the resources with which the country is so abundantly blessed. Conservation demands the welfare of this generation first, and afterward the welfare of the generation to follow."

This sounds a lot like the modern concept of "wise use." Indeed, that term apparently did originate with Pinchot, and since it has become a code phrase for clear-cutting, irresponsible mining, and overgrazing, modern habitat advocates have every right to question Pinchot's credentials as one of them. But whatever his motives, Pinchot was clearly instrumental in one of the Roosevelt administration's enduring achievements: the creation of sixty-six national forests in twenty different states, and the (admittedly less than perfect) protection of 148 million acres of public land within their boundaries. He was instrumental in helping Roosevelt shift responsibility for federal lands away from political hacks and into the hands of professionals who could manage them according to scientific principles. And he was a consistent advocate of managing federal lands for the benefit of the public rather than industry. "The conservation issue is a moral issue," he wrote, "and the heart of it is this: For whose benefit shall our natural resources be conserved—for the benefit of us all, or for the use and profit of a few?"

Muir, on the other hand, virtually defined the strict preservationist viewpoint. In simple terms, he wanted the land left alone, period. In contrast to Pinchot, Muir's contributions were more philosophical than practical (although he did convince Roosevelt to extend some specific protection to parts of Yosemite and nearby forests). He asked nothing of the land other than that it be there, and he wrote of wild places in overtly religious terms. It is fascinating to imagine just what he and Roosevelt talked about during their wilderness walkabout in 1903.

Where did Roosevelt's own views fall in the continuum between the two poles Pinchot and Muir represented? He could articulate both views according to situation and circumstance. Among other things, Roosevelt was something that Pinchot and (certainly!) Muir were not: a highly adept politician. The careful reader will note a subtle disconnection between Roosevelt's personal writing and his public policy statements on wildlife and the environment, simply because he was an intuitively political animal more interested in accomplishing his objectives than maintaining any appearance of ideological purity. "I want to go just as far in preserving the forests and preserving the game and wild creatures as I can *lead* public sentiment," he wrote. "But if I try to *drive* public sentiment I shall fail, save in exceptional cases."

George Grinnell directly addressed Roosevelt's apparently conflicting feelings about conservation versus preservation in his introduction to the 1904 *Book of the Boone and Crockett Club,* written from the perspective of a trusted colleague and old friend:

> It is not too much to say, however, that the chair of chief magistrate has never been occupied by a sportsman whose range of interests was so wide, and so actively manifested, as in the case of Mr. Roosevelt. It is true that Mr. Harrison, Mr. Cleveland, and Mr. McKinley did much in the way of setting aside forest reservations, but chiefly from economic motives; because they believed that forests should be preserved both for the timber that they might yield, if wisely exploited, and for their value as storage reservoirs for the waters of our rivers.
>
> The view taken by Mr. Roosevelt is quite different. To him, the economics of the case appeal with the same force that they might have for the hard-headed, common sense business American; but beyond this, and perhaps, if the secrets of his heart were known, more than this, Mr. Roosevelt is influenced by a love of nature, which, though considered sentimental by some, is, in fact, nothing more than far-sightedness, which looks toward the health, happiness, and general well-being of the American race for the future.

Many of Roosevelt's statements suggesting a favorable view toward at least limited development on some federal lands were designed to appease the western legislators with whom he battled throughout his term in office. On the other hand, passages from his 1905 *Pastimes of an American Hunter* could have come straight from Muir: "There can be nothing in the world more beautiful than the Yosemite, the groves of the giant sequoias and redwoods, the Canyon of the Yellowstone, and the Three Tetons; and our people should see to it that they are preserved for their children and their children's children forever, with their majestic beauty all unmarred."

Throughout his tenure in office, Roosevelt never forgot his roots as a sportsman. Trophy game heads lined the walls of the State Dining Room for visiting dignitaries to make of what they may. Presidential hunting trips became as closely watched and commented upon as golf games in subsequent administrations. Since there really was no organized anti-hunting movement at the time, Roosevelt never had to apologize or explain—though I doubt he would do so even today.

A 1902 episode illustrates the way he seamlessly blended his sporting life with his public persona while adding to the already considerable body of Roosevelt mythology. That November, Roosevelt traveled to Mississippi's Yazoo Delta to hunt bear. His geographical destination made the hunting trip a political statement, since his boldly progressive policies toward African Americans had made him deeply unpopular among southern racists. Although Roosevelt later characterized the five-day hunt as "simply exasperating," one voluntary decision *not* to kill a bear led to a national outpouring of admiration.

On the morning of November 14, hounds managed by his veteran guide Holt Collier picked up a track and yapped their way off into the swamp. Roosevelt returned to camp after losing the track, while Collier's hounds eventually bayed the bear. While several versions of the events that followed survive, it seems clear that other members of the party then led Roosevelt to the exhausted bear, which Collier had lassoed and tied to a tree. Dismayed by the bear's small size and helpless state, Roosevelt declined to shoot it, a decision that ensured his failure to kill a bear of any kind on the trip.

At a time when bears, like most large predators, were widely regarded as vermin (Collier himself had killed some 1,600 of them), Roosevelt's decision attracted considerable attention from the press as a remarkable example of sportsmanship. Noted *Washington Post* cartoonist Clifford Berryman found the image irresistible, and drew a series of cartoons using a principled Roosevelt and a helpless bear cub (which the original animal, in real life, was not) to illustrate presidential positions on a variety of political topics. Over time, Berryman's cartoon bears became progressively rounder, cuter, and more cuddly. Linked to the presidential nickname, the "Teddy Bear" was born, and the evolving concept of American sportsmanship and fair chase received an enduring boost from the White House.

The national forests (still known as "forest reserves" at the beginning of his term) that Roosevelt created with Pinchot's help were hardly the only examples of federal lands he preserved for posterity. The number of national parks doubled from five to ten during his administration and, encouraged by Muir, he laid the groundwork for Yosemite's expansion. In 1906 Roosevelt successfully guided the American Antiquities Act through Congress. This legislation allowed the creation of national monuments to protect from development federal lands with "historic landmarks, historic and prehistoric structures, and other objects of historic or scientific interest"—a mandate that Roosevelt interpreted as liberally as needed to protect whatever federal lands he considered worthy. The Roosevelt administration designated eighteen such national monuments, and his Antiquities Act provides an ongoing basis for the protection and preservation of ecologically and historically significant sites to this day.

Roosevelt's vision and overpowering personality led to a substantial expansion of executive power from the White House—a theoretically scary political development that nonetheless reaped huge benefits for wildlife and wild places. The creation of a national park, for example, required an act of Congress, and the powerful mining lobby successfully managed to block Roosevelt's efforts to provide such protection for the Grand Canyon. Following the passage of the Antiquities Act, however, Roosevelt simply declared the canyon a national monument.

Another memorable example of Roosevelt's willingness to wield executive power on behalf of wildlife arose when the Florida Audubon Society asked him to provide some form of protection for Pelican Island's bird population, which commercial plume hunters had nearly decimated. "Is there any law that will prevent me from declaring Pelican Island a Federal Bird Reservation?" he famously asked Attorney General Philander Knox in 1903. "Very well, then I so declare it." With those words, Roosevelt created the first national wildlife refuge. Fifty more followed during his administration, and, as administered by the federal Fish and Wildlife Service, the National Wildlife Refuge System provides critically important benefits to wildlife—and sportsmen—to this day.

Roosevelt created yet another mechanism for the protection of wildlife and habitat when he created the Wichita Game Preserve in 1905 and stocked it with bison in 1907. He authorized three additional game preserves during his presidency. The principal difference between the game preserves and national wildlife refuges was their funding. Initially, federal wildlife refuges had to depend on private sources of money for management and law enforcement, but Roosevelt cajoled Congress into granting appropriations that at least partially funded those services on the preserves.

Given his enthusiasm for the chase, did all these efforts to preserve wildlife reflect nothing more than self-interest on behalf of hunters? That's a legitimate question, to which the record provides a definitive answer. In the first place, Roosevelt's personal writings reveal little if any distinctions in his regard for game and non-game wildlife. Despite his obvious enthusiasm for big game animals (note his creation of the Bull Moose Party in his belated and unsuccessful attempt to win a third presidential term), the same sentiment extended to wildlife that was never any sportsman's quarry: "To lose the chance to see frigatebirds soaring in circles above the storm," he wrote, "or a file of pelicans winging their way homeward across the crimson afterglow of the sunset, or a myriad of terns flashing in the bright light of midday as they hover in a shifting maze above the beach—why, the loss is like the loss of a gallery of the masterpieces of the artists of old time."

Furthermore, his presidential actions confirmed these attitudes. No game species were at stake on Pelican Island. While what eventually became the National Wildlife Refuge System benefits both game and sportsmen today, Roosevelt's original term for those tracts of land—federal bird reservations—clearly reflects his intention to create them without regard to the sporting value of the species he meant them to protect. And while he took specific steps to protect and preserve bison in the West, two of his boldest uses of executive power on behalf of wildlife involved non-game species.

In 1906 Japanese sealers raided Saint Paul's Island in the Bering Sea and killed thousands of seals in a nominally protected rookery. An indignant Roosevelt denounced the outrage in his Sixth Annual Message to Congress, noted that such depredations had reduced the island's seal population from over four million when President Grant first declared them protected to fewer than two hundred thousand, and demanded legislation to criminalize the entry of foreign sealers into U.S. waters. To emphasize his commitment, he also announced the dispatch of a naval vessel to Saint Paul's. He acted with similar determination in 1909 when he ordered marines to Laysan Island to protect nesting shorebirds from commercial poachers. Neither boobies nor fur seals were of any intrinsic importance to sportsmen, but Roosevelt did not hesitate to use his authority to protect them by executive fiat. Speak softly and carry a big stick indeed.

One of the final enduring accomplishments of his administration took place in May 1908, when Roosevelt convened the first National Conference of Governors at the White House. The agenda focused exclusively upon conservation. Nowadays the notion of a national conference about anything may sound suspiciously like a political excuse for avoiding action on important issues, but the event was remarkable for its time. No president had ever called to order such a meeting before, and Roosevelt's choice of priorities provides a firm indication of where he believed his legacy lay in the waning days of his presidency: "You have come hither at my request, so that we may join together to consider the question of the conservation and use of the great fundamental sources of wealth of this Nation. So vital is this question, that for the first time in our history the chief executive officers of the states separately, and of the states together forming the Nation, have met to consider it. It is the chief material question that confronts us."

When Roosevelt left office nine months later, he took a logical step for a dedicated sportsman suddenly released from the responsibility of years in the country's most demanding job: He departed on an epic African safari, as recounted in his *African Game Trails* (one of the twenty-four books he wrote during his lifetime). By that time, his record of executive accomplishment was staggering. His success as a trust-buster, champion of workers' rights (the Workman's Compensation Act), and consumer safety advocate (the Pure Food and Drug Act) could have made him a liberal icon. But he also rebuilt the nation's military, turning the country into a true international power, and oversaw the construction of the Panama Canal. He was the first American to win a Nobel Prize (for brokering the peace treaty that ended the Russo-Japanese War) and the first president to invite a black man to dinner at the White House (Booker T. Washington, in October 1901).

Despite all these accomplishments, Roosevelt considered his efforts to protect the nation's wildlife and natural resources the greatest aspect of his legacy, an opinion with which many modern historians agree. Call it conservation (as he did), preservation, or more accurately a mixture of the two—Roosevelt's visionary policies rescued millions of acres of public land from the threat of exploitation and saved countless wildlife species from the ravages they had endured during the previous century. Perhaps more important than any specific piece of legislation, Roosevelt almost single-handedly shifted these issues from obscurity to the forefront of the national agenda, anticipating the modern greening of America by nearly a century. Absent Roosevelt's determination, there likely wouldn't have been much left for modern activists of any persuasion to save—a fact that the anti-hunting element of today's environmental movement would do well to note.

From 1980 until 1986 I lived in a rural home on Alaska's Kenai Peninsula. Our property line bordered the Kenai National Wildlife Refuge (which began life in 1941 as the National Moose Range, before it became politically incorrect to identify federal land with a big game species). If I were to follow a line of latitude due east from my house, I would cross just one road—the Alcan

Highway—before reaching the Labrador Sea over three thousand miles away. Moose and brown bears wandered regularly across the vista in front of our deck. A ten-minute flight in the Super Cub parked in my yard would take me over Dall sheep, mountain goats, glaciers, and arctic grayling. I—or more properly, we— owed all that to sportsman Theodore Roosevelt, who not only created the National Wildlife Refuge System but rammed legislation protecting Alaskan wildlife from commercial exploitation through Congress at a time when hardly anyone in the country could imagine why such issues mattered.

LACEY, SHIRAS, AND TWO LANDMARK LAWS

B y the mid-1800s at least some American sportsmen, virtually alone among all other segments of our society, had
begun to recognize the impending wildlife disaster gathering force all around them. In word and print, they expressed varying degrees of alarm, sadness, anger, and regret, often eloquently.
Unfortunately, most of this concern boiled down to impotent
hand-wringing as everyone waited for someone else to *do* something. Of course, it's easy to be critical in retrospect. As members
of an environmentally aware generation (at least nominally), we
forget what a recent phenomenon the greening of America's public
attitudes really is. In America during the age of Manifest Destiny,
the notion that wildlife had value distinct from whatever price it
might command on the open market seemed positively radical.

No doubt the temporal pace of wildlife's decline was one reason why American sportsmen were slower to act than to speak.
By the time the problem was apparent, it already seemed too late
to do anything about it. Indeed, a sense of helplessness pervades
much contemporary writing on the subject—even, on occasion,
Grinnell's. Once just a couple of dozen bison survived in the wild,
options to hand-wringing were hard to imagine.

Distaste for the anti-democratic provisions of traditional
British wildlife law doubtlessly contributed to sportsmen's regulatory inertia in post-Revolutionary America. While British law
benefited wildlife by securing habitat and restricting means of
take, its qualification provisions also helped limit the sporting
benefits of wildlife to members of the upper classes. After successfully fighting a war against just such elitist principles, any attempt
to limit a frontiersman's freedom to take game at will faced an
uphill battle in the court of American public opinion, even if the
game animals in question were the last buffalo standing.

American sportsmen initially lacked the tools to become effective activists. The media of the day were slow, cumbersome, and—prior to the founding of the first national sporting periodicals in the 1870s—profoundly disinterested in the subject. While the railroad industry could afford to park full-time lobbyists outside congressional doors in Washington (in congressional lobbies, actually, for that is the origin of the word), citizen activists faced significant practical obstacles to direct political action. Often individualists by nature, sportsmen were notoriously poor organizers, as they often still are today. Lone voices crying from the wilderness of small-town America, where many sportsmen lived, were easy to ignore, especially for legislators besieged by slick industry touts carrying suitcases full of cash.

But times change, and by the end of the nineteenth century, sportsmen had found their voice in a pugnacious outdoor press and organized themselves into clubs capable of wielding true political clout, if only by virtue of the wealth and connections of their members. An important 1896 Supreme Court decision, *Geer v. Connecticut,* confirmed the states' authority to regulate the taking of wildlife. At last, sportsmen began to lobby successfully for meaningful legislation to protect America's wild resources. Especially at the federal level, many of those early statutes endure as important foundations of wildlife law today.

1900—The Lacey Act

Born in Virginia in 1841, John Fletcher Lacey practiced law in Iowa after fighting with distinction in the Third Iowa Infantry during the Civil War. After serving in the Iowa legislature, he was first elected to the House of Representatives in 1889. He served there again from 1893 to 1907, including a term as chairman of the Committee on Public Lands.

An avid sportsman, Lacey befriended George Bird Grinnell and Theodore Roosevelt early during his tenure in Washington and soon became a staunch legislative ally in their budding conservation movement, a role mirrored in the other house by Illinois senator George Vest. A social as well as a political associate, Lacey was an original member of the Boone and Crockett Club.

Lacey was an early advocate of conservation measures at a time when such issues aroused little enthusiasm in Congress. By the end of his first term, he had already helped draft the legislation that created the Forest Reserve Program, the forerunner of the National Forest System (which Lacey helped Roosevelt and Gifford Pinchot create a decade later). He earned George Grinnell's everlasting gratitude by authoring the Yellowstone Park Protection Act of 1894. During his long legislative career, he was a consistent advocate of Native American rights and helped create laws protecting Indian burial grounds and other archeological sites from exploitation.

His most enduring legacy, however, is the second piece of legislation that still bears his name, originally known as the Lacey Bird Act of 1900. As the bill's title implies, it first arose in response to its author's concern for birds, which he enjoyed as a hunter, observer, and simple enthusiast of wildlife. At the time, they certainly needed his help.

The market trade in wild birds was in full swing at the close of the nineteenth century. By way of illustration, Aldo Leopold later noted that Chicago markets traded 600,000 prairie chickens at $3.25 per dozen in 1873. The small town of Spooner, Wisconsin, near Leopold's home, shipped 25,000 to market in 1896.

But by 1900, thanks to the whims of fashion and the millinery trade, the avian market extended far beyond edible game birds. Among fashionable women at the turn of the twentieth century, feathered hats became the rage. Some even included entire stuffed birds in addition to feathers; think Carmen Miranda with songbirds instead of tropical fruit. Plumes from wading birds, especially snowy egrets, became especially popular, leading commercial hunters to decimate egret and heron populations in the Everglades and elsewhere around the South. Commercial plume hunters were a ruthless lot—when Grinnell's newly formed Audubon Society eventually dispatched private guards to protect

Florida's few remaining colonies of breeding egrets, poachers killed three of the guards in the line of duty. Other species were vulnerable as well, including gulls and terns, and commercial hunters decimated entire nesting colonies of them. In 1884 one New York broker shipped forty thousand tern skins to a Paris millinery at 10 cents per feathered hide.

Fortunately for wildlife, Lacey was astute enough to draft the bill in general terms, so that its provisions extended beyond wild birds. Its central provision made it unlawful for any person to "import, export, sell, receive, acquire, or purchase any fish or wildlife or plant taken, possessed, transported, or sold in violation of any law, treaty, or regulation of the United States or in violation of any Indian tribal law" (in the current language of the act).

Coming at a time when individual states were finally beginning to draft meaningful wildlife protection statutes, particularly with regard to the market trade in meat, hides, and feathers, this simple language carried tremendous implications. If Florida passed a law protecting snowy egrets, it was no longer just a violation of Florida state law to kill them—it was also a violation of federal law to ship them to Philadelphia, receive them in Baltimore, or turn them into hats in New York. As state legislatures passed progressively more protective wildlife laws over the course of the next two decades, the Lacey Act largely eliminated the commercial trade in illegal wildlife.

President William McKinley signed the bill into law in 1900. By the time of its first major application, McKinley had been assassinated and Theodore Roosevelt occupied the White House.

In 1909 a feather merchant hired twenty-three Japanese laborers to sail to Laysan Island and collect wings from nesting seabirds like the Laysan albatross, which they exported in violation of the Lacey Act. (A remote extension of the Hawaiian Island chain, Laysan was an American territory at the time. We now know it as Midway after its critical geographic role in the battle for the Pacific after the Japanese attack on Pearl Harbor.) Awkward and essentially helpless when nesting on land, the birds made easy prey, and the poachers killed some three hundred thousand of them over the course of two months. A zoologist in Honolulu heard of the slaughter and notified federal authorities. Roosevelt dispatched a naval cutter to the scene, where marines apprehended the poachers and brought them back to Hawaii for trial.

Later that year, Roosevelt issued an executive order creating the Hawaiian Islands Reservation for Birds, which included Laysan Island. Today, the island is administered by the Fish and Wildlife Service and provides critical breeding ground for the Laysan albatross and other pelagic bird species, as well as the endangered Hawaiian monk seal, illustrating how a well-crafted piece of wildlife legislation can have far-reaching influence a century after its passage.

Congress has tweaked the Lacey Act several times. A 1969 amendment expanded its scope to include reptiles, amphibians, mollusks, and crustaceans. In 1981 Congress lowered the act's standard of proof from "willfully" to "knowingly," increased penalties, and allowed for warrantless arrests by federal agents. In 1988 the scope of the law was expanded again to include illegal commercial guiding and outfitting businesses. But the core provisions of the law have remained unchanged for over a century, and legal authorities consider it a cornerstone of federal wildlife law enforcement today.

John Lacey was savvy enough to realize that meaningful protection of wildlife required new attitudes as well as new laws, and he never hesitated to pursue the cause. Addressing the Iowa Federation of Women's Clubs in 1905, he got right in his hostesses' faces after a few benign opening remarks. "In the preservation of our birds, the women of America were slow to act," he chided, "but now they are doing a great part. We have a wireless telegraph, a crownless queen, a thornless cactus, a seedless orange, and a coreless apple. Let us now have a birdless hat!" Someone was listening—the federation went on to become a staunch supporter of conservation causes.

Given the mindless antipathy that too often arises between hunting and non-hunting wildlife advocates today, it should probably come as no surprise to hear the Lacey Act referenced as an example of sound anti-hunting legislation. Nothing could be further from the truth, with regard to both the bill's results and its original intent. As for the latter, one only need consider Lacey's own remarks when he first introduced his landmark bill in Congress: "I have always been a lover of birds; and I have always been a hunter as well; for today there is no friend that the birds have like the true sportsman—the man who enjoys legitimate sport. He protects them out of season; he kills them in moderation in season."

Thanks to some farsighted politicking, sportsman John Lacey is still protecting them nearly a century after his death in 1913.

1918—The Migratory Bird Treaty Act

Despite its importance both as historic precedent and a practical legal weapon against the commercial wildlife trade, the Lacey Act suffered an important shortcoming: In order to be prosecuted under its provisions, a violator had to break another wildlife law. The act was primarily designed to impede interstate traffic in illegally harvested wildlife, but at the time, state laws governing wildlife were a chaotic patchwork of statutes ranging from ambitious to nonexistent. The problem of uniform legal jurisdiction for wildlife was especially critical in the case of migratory populations of birds that lived their lives without regard to arbitrary legal boundaries.

The first federal legislative attempt to address these matters came in 1913, with the passage of the Weeks-McLean Law. This act spelled out an ambitious expansion of federal regulation over certain wildlife: "All wild geese, wild swans, brant, wild ducks, snipe, plover, woodcock, rail, wild pigeons" (never mind that the wild pigeons were already dead) and "all other migratory game and insectivorous birds which in their northern and southern migrations pass through or do not remain permanently the entire year within the borders of a State or Territory shall hereafter be deemed to be within the custody and protection of the Government of the

United States, and shall not be destroyed or taken contrary to regulations hereinafter provided."

The law suffered legal and political flaws from the outset. Passed as a rider to an Agriculture Department appropriations bill, it lacked broad congressional support, and poorly worded language elsewhere in the bill made it vulnerable to an immediate legal challenge on the grounds of states' rights violations. Rather than fight battles they were likely to lose, its supporters went back to the drawing board.

As in the case of the Lacey Act, successful early wildlife legislation usually depended on the persistence of a few highly motivated individuals. In the case of the Migratory Bird Treaty Act (MBTA) of 1918, the key player was George Shiras III. Early wildlife advocates tended to be Renaissance men whose talents extended across a wide range of interests, and Shiras was no exception. Indeed, Ernest Hemingway once labeled him in print "about the most interesting man I know."

Born in 1859 to a distinguished family (his father, George Shiras Jr., served as a Supreme Court justice), Shiras developed a passion for the wild as a boy in the woods of northern Michigan. He hunted avidly as a young man, although he eventually gave up his rifle in favor of the camera. An innovative outdoor photographer, he pioneered the use of flash systems for nighttime wildlife photography. When the staid (and previously image-free) *National Geographic* devoted an issue to his photographs in 1906, society board member Alfred Brooks (for whom Alaska's Brooks Range is named) resigned in protest, claiming that editor Gilbert Grosvenor was turning the publication into "a picture book."

Too busy to be a politician, Shiras only served one term in Congress, from 1903 to 1905. During that term, he drafted legislation creating Olympic National Park and authored and introduced the original version of the bill that would eventually become the MBTA over a decade later.

The legal impetus for the resurrection of Shiras's stalled legislation was a 1916 treaty with Canada prohibiting the transport of illegally taken migratory birds between the two countries. To satisfy terms of the treaty, Congress needed to provide legislation unifying the states' chaotic waterfowl harvest regulations, a basis critical to the act's eventual legal challenge. The MBTA granted broad federal authority to regulate the taking and transport of a long list of migratory bird species, including their eggs and feathers. While the act has been subject to numerous minor amendments and modifications over time, its core principle—that the federal government has the jurisdiction and authority to oversee the welfare of migratory bird populations—remains unchanged.

In conjunction with the provisions of the Lacey Act, the MBTA effectively halted market hunting for waterfowl. Today, hunters recognize its intent every fall as the U.S. Fish and Wildlife Service determines and enforces hunting regulations for waterfowl and other migratory game birds. However, the act's provisions extend to numerous non-game species as well, and they protect birds from environmental mishaps as well as overhunting.

Like the Weeks-McClean Law before it, the MBTA faced inevitable constitutional challenge. Shortly after its passage, the state of Missouri filed suit to prevent federal game wardens from enforcing the act on grounds of interference with states' rights to manage wildlife. In its 1920 *Missouri v. Holland* decision, the Supreme Court ruled the MBTA constitutional, "establishing beyond question the supremacy of the Federal treaty-making power as a source of authority for Federal wildlife regulation."

Even though George Shiras exchanged firearms for cameras during the latter part of his life, he worked together with active hunters to craft the basis for this vital piece of legislation and remained a friend and associate of many well-known sportsmen throughout his life. He eventually heeded Theodore Roosevelt's plea to turn his wildlife notes and photographs into a "big book," and the National Geographic Society published his *Hunting Wildlife with Camera and Flashlight* in 1935. Despite the importance of his early wildlife legislation, sportsmen today remember him best for the eponym he provided the distinctive subspecies of moose that inhabits the western United States, *Alces alces shirasii*.

By the 1920s American wildlife in general and waterfowl in particular had apparently turned the corner, snatched back from the brink by legislative action spearheaded by a handful of visionary advocates, almost all of whom were sportsmen. The intent of much of this legislation, including the Lacey Act and Migratory Bird Treaty Act, was to salvage wildlife from predation by commercial market hunters. As important as these laws proved to be, they did not address all the ways in which human activity could adversely impact wildlife, by design or accident.

Expansion and development were eating away at the pristine habitat Lewis and Clark described more rapidly than ever before. Prosperity and rapidly evolving technology were inventing new and more devastating means of threatening the places where wildlife lived. While many concerned sportsmen breathed a collective sigh of relief at the collapse of the market hunting industry, vanishing habitat represented a new threat on the horizon that most Americans failed to appreciate simply because our country's supply of wild places had so recently seemed limitless.

The drought of the Dust Bowl era was about to turn an abstract threat into an immediate crisis. The ways sportsmen found to respond to it determined the course that wildlife advocacy would take for the rest of the century and beyond, by hunters and non-hunters alike.

SAVING WATERFOWL: THE 1930S

The economic ravages of the Great Depression and war clouds gathering abroad made the 1930s trying times for most Americans and their wildlife, including the country's ducks and geese. While the continent's waterfowl began the decade in desperate circumstances, the '30s ultimately proved beneficial to them, for those difficult years produced key developments crucial to their survival into the century ahead.

By this time, the legal provisions of the Migratory Bird Treaty and Lacey Acts had largely eliminated market hunting for ducks. Continental waterfowl numbers were just beginning to recover from decades of commercial overharvest when a new crisis arose in a form that, for once, was not entirely due to human activities. Drought struck, and the same Dust Bowl conditions that sent farms into foreclosure all across the Midwest decimated midcontinental waterfowl breeding habitat. Sportsmen had no sooner saved the birds from the ravages of human folly than natural events threatened to undo their efforts. (Not that nature was entirely to blame. Draining wetlands in largely unsuccessful attempts to increase agricultural production during a period of high grain prices seriously amplified the effects of the drought.) And no one has ever been able to draft legislation capable of making rain fall from the sky.

These were challenging times for waterfowl and their advocates, but the most difficult problems often produce the most imaginative solutions. By its conclusion, the decade had produced several developments of lasting importance not just to waterfowl, but to all American wildlife.

Ding Darling and the Federal Duck Stamp

Once again, sportsmen were the first to recognize the impending crisis. Because waterfowl migrate freely across jurisdictional boundaries, policies implemented solely at the state level were clearly inadequate, and concerned sportsmen turned to the federal government for leadership in the restoration of crucial waterfowl habitat. Their early lobbying efforts came with an important provision nearly without precedent: willingness to pay their own way for what they wanted. Seventy years later, how many more interest groups have approached Congress with both a request *and* a commitment to pick up the tab?

Once again, farsighted wildlife legislation arose because of the efforts of one determined sportsman. The principal driving force behind the effort to save North American waterfowl during this critical time came from Jay "Ding" Darling, a Pulitzer Prize–winning editorial cartoonist for the *Des Moines Register* and avid duck hunter. After Darling demonstrated admirable leadership at the state level by helping to organize an innovative program for funding wildlife management in Iowa, President Franklin Delano Roosevelt named him to serve on a special committee convened to study the wetlands crisis, along with Aldo Leopold and Tom Beck, the chair of the Connecticut Board of Fisheries and Game. While the committee came up with a number of far-reaching proposals, no appropriations were available from the cash-strapped Depression-era administration. Working with Senator Fredric Wolcott, chair of the first Senate Committee on Conservation of Wildlife Resources and a member of the Boone and Crockett Club's Executive Committee, Darling crafted a unique funding proposal.

The Migratory Bird Hunting Stamp Act became law in 1934, creating what has been popularly known ever since as the duck stamp. (Congress changed its official name to the Migratory Bird Hunting and Conservation Stamp in 1976.) The law required all hunters over age sixteen to purchase a federal duck stamp in addition to any required state licenses and permits in order to hunt waterfowl anywhere in the nation. The original stamp cost

$1. (That amount has risen seven times since 1934, to its current price of $15.)

The act also stipulated that all revenues from duck stamp sales go directly to the Migratory Bird Conservation Fund rather than disappearing into the federal treasury. Darling lobbied hard for this provision after noting that state revenues from license sales almost always vanished into general revenue funds, where they did hunters and wildlife little good. Furthermore, not less than 90 percent of the revenue collected through duck stamp sales had to be used by the U.S. Fish and Wildlife Service for the "purchase, development, and maintenance" of waterfowl refuges, with the remaining 10 percent used for administration and enforcement. (Subsequent amendments have altered those percentages. Currently, 98 percent of all duck stamp revenues are earmarked for the purchase or lease and subsequent protection of wetlands habitat.)

It would be difficult to overstate the success of this legislation. Duck stamp sales have netted over $700 million for wetlands conservation and funded the acquisition of 5.2 million acres of crucial wildlife habitat by the National Wildlife Refuge System. While anyone is free to purchase a federal duck stamp and a few non-hunters do, the overwhelming majority of those revenues derive from sportsmen. Many duck hunters buy several extra stamps every year as a convenient means of making additional contributions to wildlife habitat.

Widely regarded as one of the most successful conservation programs in the world, the Duck Stamp Act (as it is popularly known) has produced numerous benefits above and beyond the production of more game for hunters. The stamp itself has certainly served the cause of wildlife art. Every year a spirited competition leads to the selection of the winning waterfowl portrait for the new edition of the stamp. A Junior Duck Stamp competition encourages young artists to participate along with the most respected wildlife painters in the country. While there is no direct monetary reward in either contest, artists are free to sell reproductions of the winning entry, and the prestige and publicity that come from having one's work selected can make a career in wildlife art. No doubt the duck stamp has helped make waterfowl one of the genre's most popular subjects.

The refuges that duck stamp revenues have saved from development benefit far more wildlife than waterfowl alone. Since refuge sites are selected from wetlands strategically situated along major migratory flyways, other migratory aquatic birds are obvious beneficiaries, including plovers, sandpipers, curlews, and cranes, just to name a few. The endangered whooping cranes that winter at Texas's Aransas National Wildlife Refuge owe no small measure of their security to duck hunters. Prime habitat and abundant birdlife in turn support healthy populations of predators. The refuges are important to entire ecosystems beyond their boundaries, and not just because they provide secure stopping points for migrating birds. Undisturbed wetlands improve the quality of the water table, and the refuges secure millions of acres of land against development of any kind.

At Roosevelt's request, Darling himself designed the nation's first duck stamp in 1934. Somewhat unsophisticated by the stamp's later standards, the image, which shows two mallard settling onto a pond, betrays Darling's own artistic background in the inadvertently cartoonish appearance of the birds' bills which, upon close inspection, betray unfortunate suggestions of Donald Duck. Nonetheless, it went on to become one of the most widely reproduced wildlife images of all time.

Later in 1934, Roosevelt named Darling to head the U.S. Biological Survey, the forerunner of the U.S. Fish and Wildlife Service. In that capacity, Darling acted aggressively to restore threatened flights of ducks and geese. While the heyday of the market hunter was long past, significant commercial poaching rings still operated openly in California and on Maryland's Eastern Shore, and illegal spring shooting was still common along the Mississippi flyway. With a total of just twenty-four agents scattered about the entire country, Darling's agency clearly lacked the resources to enforce the law. As an interim measure, Darling organized his agents into mobile undercover units aided by sportsmen and local law enforcement officers temporarily commissioned as federal agents. While his "phantom squads" enjoyed spectacular successes against the most blatant poachers, Darling went to work producing more wildlife professionals.

When Darling was still in Iowa, he had spearheaded a far-reaching proposal to remove the state's Conservation Department from political influence and replace it with a nonpartisan commission, the first such effort in the country. One of the commission's first accomplishments was the creation of a fish and wildlife training school at Iowa State University. Encouraged by the program's success, Darling set out to reproduce it at the national level. He proposed funding similar programs at nine other land grant colleges and secured partial funding from the schools and state conservation departments, but still lacked the financing to complete the project.

In the spring of 1934, Darling organized a meeting of interested private parties and secured the necessary financial backing for his education initiative from representatives of the sporting industry, including DuPont, Hercules Powder, and Remington Arms. As another beneficial outcome of that meeting, participants laid the groundwork for the formation of the American Wildlife Institute, which became an umbrella organization that eventually united several thousand state and local sportsmen's groups behind the common cause of wildlife and habitat conservation and evolved into the North American Wildlife Foundation.

In 1935 Darling used his authority as head of the Biological Survey to create a number of important regulations to minimize hunters' impact on imperiled waterfowl populations, including harsh restrictions on seasons and bag limits—measures that did not have to last indefinitely. He also outlawed the use of bait, live decoys, and shotguns capable of holding more than three shells, all appropriate ethical restrictions that endure to this day.

Although Darling only served eighteen months as chief of the Biological Survey, his drive and organizational ability made this a period of remarkable accomplishment. His integrity and commitment to wildlife allowed him the rare ability to function effectively across traditional Washington political lines. (Although appointed to his position by FDR, Darling was a lifelong Republican who had frequently taken the New Deal to task during his days as a political cartoonist in Des Moines.) After retiring from federal service in 1935, he became the first president of the National Wildlife Federation and remained active in conservation causes until his death in 1962.

The Pittman-Robertson Act

Like most idealistic political ventures, the field of wildlife management and habitat restoration has always been long on ideas and short on funds. The success of the innovative federal Duck Stamp Act confirmed an important principle: Sportsmen were quite willing to underwrite programs that benefited the wildlife they enjoyed as long as the funds they contributed were used wisely for their intended purpose. While the Duck Stamp Act was well received and provided immediate benefits for waterfowl, many members of the sporting community recognized the need to provide similar sources of stable funding for the benefit of other varieties of wildlife. They soon realized their goal.

In 1930 Connecticut senator Fredric Walcott, a longstanding legislative champion of sporting and conservation causes, called for and obtained a special bicameral committee on wildlife. By 1934 the Special Committee on the Conservation of Wildlife Resources consisted of seven members of the Senate, chaired by Senator Key Pittman of Nevada, and seven representatives of the House, led by Representative A. Willis Robertson of Virginia. (Both Pittman and Robertson were enthusiastic sportsmen themselves.) To help finance Roosevelt's New Deal, Congress had already restored previously lapsed federal excise taxes on a number of items, including firearms and ammunition. However, there was no direct relationship between funds generated by taxes on sporting goods and monies spent on wildlife or conservation.

At the 1937 North American Wildlife Conference, the newly formed National Wildlife Federation (a sportsmen's group)

lamented the lack of funding for important conservation initiatives and proposed a means of legislative relief. At the federation's
urging, Pittman and Robertson introduced identical bills in the
House and Senate later that year whose eventual passage has had
a tremendous beneficial impact on wildlife ever since.

The Federal Aid in Wildlife Restoration Act (popularly known
as the Pittman-Robertson Act, or simply P-R) earmarked funds
derived from the 10 percent federal excise tax on firearms and
ammunition (subsequently raised to 11 percent) for distribution
to state and territorial wildlife agencies, to be used specifically
for wildlife habitat acquisition, development, and research. The
federal government was allowed to keep 8 percent of revenues to
fund administration of the program, while the remainder went
directly to the states. However, to qualify for the receipt of those
federal funds, states had to do two things, as all states eventually
did: match the federal funds at a 25 to 75 percent ratio, and pass
an enabling act prohibiting the state from diverting those funds
to any account other than its fish and wildlife agency's. The latter
provision addressed a common practice detrimental to wildlife:
redirecting sportsmen's dollars derived from license sales and other
sources to fund unrelated state pork-barrel projects. Allocation to
the states was based on a formula that considered both the size of
the state and the number of hunting licenses it sold.

Like most prototype wildlife legislation, Pittman-Robertson
faced challenges (including an early attempt at repeal successfully
lobbied against by sportsmen who could already see tangible results
from the bill) and underwent inevitable tweaking, mostly for the
better: its 1951 promotion to "permanent appropriations" status, to
keep Congress from withholding funds from the trust account; the
1970 inclusion of revenue from the special federal excise tax on hand-
guns into the P-R fund; and the 1972 addition of archery equipment
to the list of taxable items. In 1950 passage of the Dingell-Johnson
Act created a similar excise tax on certain fishing tackle, with funds
directed toward wildlife habitat using P-R as a model.

Since its passage in 1937, Pittman-Robertson has directed
over $2 billion to state fish and wildlife agencies. These funds

have led to the outright purchase of over four million acres of critical wildlife habitat, and improved management for wildlife on fifty million more. Formal research in wildlife biology, a limited field at best when Pittman-Robertson became law, has subsequently blossomed at both the state and federal level, and the vast majority of funding for this training and study has derived from P-R dollars. Most analysts agree that Pittman-Robertson, like the Duck Stamp Act, is one of the most effective pieces of legislation Congress has ever passed on behalf of wildlife.

Of course, there is a certain irony in the Pittman-Robertson Act's success, with particular regard to the thesis of this book. The wildlife and habitat that have benefited from these badly needed funds are there for all to enjoy—bird-watchers, photographers, students and teachers, nature lovers of every persuasion—yet sportsmen alone have picked up the hefty tab. Have any "non-consumptive user" wildlife groups volunteered to match this effort by lobbying Congress to impose a similar excise tax on cameras, binoculars, backpacks, and hiking boots for similar purposes? We're still waiting.

In an interview with preeminent wildlife biologist Dr. Valerius Geist, I asked him to identify sportsmen's most significant contribution to wildlife. "Generating earmarked revenues for wildlife conservation!" he replied without hesitation. It all started with Pittman-Robertson.

Getting Organized

The "Alphabet Soup" of FDR's New Deal is often cited as a model of Big Government confusion and inefficiency at its worst. In fairness, critics might look at what was happening in the private sector's concurrent attempts to improve wildlife management. During the period under discussion, national players in the sportsman-driven conservation movement included the American Wild Fowlers, the More Game Birds in America Foundation, the Cooperative Wildlife Research Unit Program, the American Wildlife Institute, the American Game Protective and Propagation Association, and the North American Wildlife Foundation—not to mention some six thousand state and local groups with like goals and members of similar backgrounds.

Ding Darling and Fredric Walcott, among other national leaders, recognized the inefficiency and lack of political clout in all this duplication and called for the creation of an umbrella organization to unify the sportsman's voice in Washington. At the first North American Wildlife Conference in 1935, Darling proposed such an organization, composed of component chapters representing individual states. Within months of his proposal, twenty-five states had unified their local clubs into one state organization, and the National Wildlife Federation was born from their association. When he retired from the Biological Survey that November, Darling became its first president.

With the exception of the Wildlife Federation, which grew into a powerful and respected voice for wildlife interests, none of the organizations mentioned earlier has survived, at least in its original form. From a purely political standpoint, that is likely just as well. However, one complex historical thread weaving through that list warrants comment. In May 1931 American Wild Fowlers closed shop and turned its assets over to the newly formed More Game Birds in America Foundation. In 1937 that foundation in turn reorganized and emerged as Ducks Unlimited. After the Second World War, Ducks Unlimited became the prototype sportsman-driven, species-focused, habitat-advocacy organization and served as a model for the many similarly oriented organizations that do so much for wildlife today. I mention the organization's origins here simply because no discussion of American wildlife during the 1930s is complete without acknowledging it.

Despite the many challenges of the times, the 1930s produced landmark advances on behalf of wildlife in the form of legislation and organization, all largely driven by sportsmen. The decade also represented the high point in the career of yet another remarkable individual outdoorsman, who almost single-handedly developed the modern discipline of wildlife science as we now know it: Aldo Leopold.

Aldo Leopold and the Land Ethic

Conservation is a state of harmony between men and land. By land is meant all the things on, over, or in the earth. Harmony with land is like harmony with a friend: you cannot cherish his right hand and chop off his left. That is to say, you cannot love game and hate predators; you cannot conserve the waters and waste the ranges; you cannot build the forest and mine the farm," wrote Aldo Leopold in *Round River.*

It is interesting to contrast this definition of conservation with the views on the same subject Gifford Pinchot articulated a generation earlier. Could Pinchot and Leopold, both men acknowledged as pioneering authorities in the fields of forestry and conservation, really have been talking about the same thing? And based solely upon their definitions of conservation, which of the two would the naive observer be more likely to identify as the hunter? The comparison illustrates the folly of trying to pigeonhole modern wildlife advocates as "conservationists" or "preservationists" (or anything else). It also presages the monumental shift in American attitudes toward wildlife that began in the 1930s and eventually evolved into the ecological awareness of today. And it's discouraging to realize how many contemporary environmental activists fail to realize that it all started with a sportsman.

Today, the wildlife advocacy field almost seems overcrowded. The American Wildlife Federation's *Conservation Directory* devotes over six hundred pages just to the names and contact information of hundreds of organizations with memberships ranging from less than a thousand to over a million. Some are devoted to specific wildlife species, others to specific regions of the country and the world. They represent hunters, non-hunters, and anti-hunters, and their agendas range from the pastoral to the militant. Wildlife now has a lot of voices raised in its behalf, even if the net result often sounds more like white noise than music.

In contrast, almost all of the American conservation movement's key accomplishments during the critical period from the opening of the West until the Second World War arose, or at least began, with individual effort. No review of the subject would be complete without examining the life and work of Aldo Leopold.

Leopold was born in Iowa in 1882 to a comfortably middle-class family of German immigrants. An avid outdoorsman, his father, Carl, expressed dismay at the declining numbers of game bird species subject to commercial exploitation, such as passenger pigeons, prairie chickens, and waterfowl. By the time his sons began to hunt, Carl, a man ahead of his time, had developed his own code of ethics in the field, complete with seasons and bag limits even though there were still no such laws officially in effect. Carl Leopold eventually became an outspoken opponent of all commercial hunting and was instrumental in the creation of Iowa's first fish and game laws.

Young Aldo Leopold, like Grinnell and Roosevelt before him, spent a tremendous amount of his childhood outdoors, hunting and fishing but also observing, describing, and collecting wildlife. After completing his primary education at a private school in New Jersey, he entered Yale in 1905. In 1909 he received a master's degree in forestry, a virtually nonexistent field of study in American universities until Gifford Pinchot's ascendancy in the Roosevelt White House. In fact, Pinchot himself had attended Yale and was endowing its forestry program while Leopold studied there.

Officially a forester, Leopold traveled to the Southwest as an employee of the Agriculture Department's newly created Division of Forestry. After a rough start trying to supervise experienced timber cruisers who knew more about the terrain than he did, Leopold became instrumental in instituting a grazing permit system in New Mexico's Carson National Forest, a mission that required him to confront rough-and-tumble ranchers accustomed to grazing their livestock wherever they damn well pleased.

By 1915 Leopold had married the exotic local beauty Estella Bergere, started a family, inauspiciously begun a literary career by editing and writing for an in-house forestry publication called *The Pine Cone,* survived a near-lethal kidney ailment despite local physicians' best efforts to the contrary, and assumed responsibility for recreational policy in the Forest Service's vast southwestern District 3. While that job title may have sounded like little more than an excuse for collecting a government paycheck, Leopold took it seriously.

After months of firsthand research, he produced a game handbook for district personnel, significant both as Leopold's first written work on wildlife management and the first work of its kind the Forest Service produced. As the handbook's scope makes clear, Leopold was already thinking outside the proverbial box: "North America, in its natural state, possessed the richest fauna in the world. Its stock of game has reduced 98%. Eleven species have been already exterminated, and twenty-five more are now candidates for oblivion. Nature was a million years, or more, in developing a species . . . Man, with all his wisdom, has not evolved so much as a ground squirrel, a sparrow or a clam."

The shift in emphasis from counting trees to conserving wildlife meant new challenges for Leopold, since the whole notion of conservation was still alien to the frontier mentality of the Southwest. To muster support for his controversial new policies, he turned to local sportsmen. He traveled throughout New Mexico lecturing to sportsmen's groups about the need to end the unrestricted killing of wildlife and enforce game laws. Leopold himself expressed surprise at the enthusiasm that greeted him. In 1916 he and Miles Burford, a sportsman from Silver City, New Mexico, organized the state's outdoor clubs into the New Mexico Game Protective Association (NMGPA). With over a thousand highly motivated members in a sparsely populated state, it immediately became a significant political lobby on behalf of wildlife.

Two of the new group's immediate agenda items seem worthwhile today: vigorous enforcement of game laws and the creation of game refuges within the National Forest System. The third is more problematic: predator control. With the enthusiastic support of local stockmen, the NMGPA advocated the "wise control" of a long list of perceived enemies of wildlife (and livestock), including wolves, mountain lions, coyotes, bears, bobcats, foxes, and birds of prey. (Note that today almost all entries on that hit list are either strictly protected or managed as valuable game animals.) Remarkably in light of his views as they eventually evolved, Leopold supported this position.

To its credit, though, the NMGPA, with Leopold frequently acting as spokesman, successfully influenced state politics, while New Mexico's game laws and enforcement system developed to become among the most progressive in the nation. In 1917 Leopold received a personal message of support and congratulations from Theodore Roosevelt. Despite the importance of his later work to the future of American wildlife, Leopold never again engaged in direct political activism as he did in New Mexico.

In 1919 Leopold assumed the position of chief of operations for the Forest Service in the Southwest, overseeing some twenty million acres of public land. During his tenure he laid the groundwork for the creation of the nation's first wilderness area, did novel work on the study of soil erosion due to human activities, became one of the first foresters to question the wisdom of suppressing natural fires, wrote prolifically, and spent a lot of time hunting. He also used for the first time in print a word virtually unheard of among foresters and wildlife managers of the day: ecology. While he did not invent the term (it first appeared in the writings of an obscure German naturalist named Ernst Haeckel sixty years earlier), Leopold would eventually do as much as anyone else to make it a household word in this country.

Writing in 1924, Leopold emphasized the complex interactions among multiple human factors affecting the health of the forests. He argued that in their natural state, periodic fires caused by lightning eliminated brush and allowed grass to grow in the understory. Overgrazing by livestock eliminated the grass, allowing brush like manzanita to grow in its place, and promoting downstream erosion. Fire suppression allowed the brush to accumulate into a dangerous fuel load, promoting ever more dangerous fires in the future. At the time, the suggestion that fire could be more beneficial to forests than livestock grazing sounded as radical as it was politically provocative. And understanding the reasoning behind it practically defined the budding science of ecology, which emphasized the interrelation of multiple species together with their environment.

In May 1924, to the openly expressed dismay of local sportsmen, Leopold left the Southwest to assume a new position with the federal Forest Products Laboratory in Madison, Wisconsin. Although approaching middle age at the time of the move, so much of Leopold's important work took place in Wisconsin that he has become indelibly identified with that state.

While his work in the Forest Products Laboratory was largely limited to dry subjects like reducing wastage in the timber industry, he enjoyed considerable freedom to address other topics. Over the next several years, he helped the newly formed Izaak Walton League (a sportsmen's organization) initiate conservation initiatives to save Wisconsin's forests and waterways, consulted on habitat management on numerous federal properties, and wrote extensively for both the popular and scientific press. His writing began to question the scientific wisdom of the government's aggressive predator-elimination policies and reflected his increasing enthusiasm for the concept of preserving pure wilderness for its own sake. As a practical expression of the latter concern, Leopold was instrumental in working with the Izaak Walton League to secure wilderness designation for the portion of the Superior National Forest that would eventually become the Boundary Waters Canoe Area.

In 1928 Leopold left government service to accept a position with the Sporting Arms and Ammunition Manufacturers' Institute (SAAMI), which offered to fund a national survey of game conditions. After establishing to his satisfaction (and that of most critics of the study) that industry funding would not compromise the integrity of the science, Leopold agreed to head the project. By 1929 he had completed studies in Michigan,

Minnesota, Iowa, Ohio, Mississippi, Illinois, Indiana, and finally Wisconsin. Although this mission sounds tame today, it represented the nation's first systematic effort to bring scientific principles to bear on the study of wild game.

Leopold's reports did not hesitate to identify political as well as biological problems in the states he surveyed, and his insistence upon the primacy of habitat considerations in determining the health of game populations was revolutionary at the time. As he wrote in his Ohio survey: "The basic reason why the current system fails . . . is that it deals with stocks only, and ignores the preservation and improvement of environments. Now that accidentally favorable environments no longer prevail, they must be deliberately made favorable, or game conservation will fail."

Despite the hectic pace of his work, Leopold remained an avid sportsman. In 1926 he discovered archery, largely through the influence of Saxton Pope's recently published classic, *Hunting with the Bow and Arrow*. The whole Leopold family became avid archers, and Aldo and his sons made several bow hunting trips to the Gila Wilderness in the Southwest. Long a capable craftsman, Leopold became a skilled bowyer and made most of the family's archery equipment himself.

Among his accomplishments during his tenure with SAAMI, Leopold oversaw the creation of academic fellowships at several major midwestern universities dedicated to the study of controversies in the emerging field of wildlife biology, the first of their kind. He was also instrumental in drafting the game policy statement approved at the Seventeenth American Game Conference held in New York in 1930. Emphasizing the public ownership of wildlife and the democratic basis for American wildlife management, that position paper guided wildlife policy for decades and eventually provided the basis for the North American Model of Wildlife Conservation.

The Depression cost Leopold his funding from SAAMI, and he became officially unemployed in 1932. Living off the family savings, he used the time to complete work on his first major book, *Game Management*. The first comprehensive synthesis of emerging ecological principles as they applied to the active management of wild game, the book remains a classic in its field. And Leopold's willingness to confront political and philosophical issues above and beyond raw science assured the text an audience far beyond the arcane world of academics.

While no one recognized as much at the time, Leopold was articulating the basis for the eventual greening of America when he wrote: "In fact, twenty centuries of 'progress' have brought the average citizen a vote, a national anthem, a Ford, a bank account, and a high opinion of himself, but not the capacity to live in high density without befouling and denuding his environment, not a conviction that such capacity, rather than such density, is the true test of whether he is civilized. The practice of game management may be one of the means of developing a culture that will meet this test."

Reflecting the importance of childhood experience to the work of many modern conservation icons, Leopold dedicated the book to his father, identifying him as a "pioneer in sportsmanship."

In 1933, while still on a hiatus between day jobs, Leopold presented a seminal paper to the southwest division of the American Academy for the Advancement of Science titled "The Conservation Ethic." Having already established that the proper management of game was indistinguishable from the proper management of its habitat, Leopold now introduced an even more far-reaching theme to the discussion, arguing that management of the land should not only be guided by scientific principle rather than mere expediency, but by ethical principles as well: "There is as yet no ethic dealing with man's relationship to land and to the non-human animals and plants which grow upon it . . . Individual thinkers since the days of Ezekiel and Isaiah have asserted that the despoliation of the land is not only inexpedient but wrong. Society, however, has not yet affirmed their belief. I regard the present conservation movement as the embryo of such affirmation."

Refined over time, the views Leopold expressed in this paper eventually formed the basis for his concept of the Land Ethic, perhaps his most lasting contribution to the fields of conservation, ecology, and sportsmanship alike (although Leopold himself rarely used the term in print).

Later that year the University of Wisconsin made Leopold the country's first Professor of Game Management. (Of note, most of the behind-the-scenes lobbying for the creation of this position on Leopold's behalf came from a group of well-connected Madison sportsmen.) Acknowledged as one of the country's most progressive institutions, the university would provide Leopold a professional home for the rest of his life.

By 1934 Leopold was serving on FDR's Committee on Wildlife Restoration with Ding Darling and Tom Beck and teaching Game Management 118, a course that would eventually play a central role in producing an entire generation of wildlife biologists.

As always, Leopold found time to spend in the field. In 1934 Wisconsin held the nation's first archery-only deer season, and the Leopolds were enthusiastic participants. Local newspapers interviewed Estella Leopold prior to the hunt. Aldo, Estella, and their older sons, Starker and Luna, spent four days stalking deer in Sauk County, killing none. However, the family enjoyed the outing so much that Leopold bought an abandoned farm in the area the following year. The Leopolds eventually built a cabin on the property ("The Shack"), which became a beloved family retreat and, eventually, the setting for Leopold's most enduring literary work, *A Sand County Almanac*.

By 1936 Leopold had played a crucial role in the founding of both the Wilderness Society and the Wildlife Society and traveled extensively in Germany studying European land management practices. (He gave the latter mixed reviews.) Leopold's writing began to reflect more interest in non-game wildlife, and the term *wildlife* began to replace *game* in his work. In contrast to his own earlier positions, he became a vocal critic of deliberately eliminating predators from the wild. And while he still made regular extended hunting trips, he also began to devote more personal time to his property in the Sand Hills.

In 1938 Leopold unilaterally altered his university position title from Professor of Game Management to Professor of Wildlife

Management. The change reflected his growing recognition of the importance of all species in a given habitat to the health of game populations, and not a retreat from his enthusiasm for outdoor sport. He spent the fall bow hunting deer on his own property and hunting waterfowl and upland game with family and friends. The following year, Game Management 118 became Wildlife Ecology 118, and Leopold officially became chairman of the university's Department of Wildlife Management. He was also the department's only member.

By 1940 Leopold was heavily involved in a major waterfowl research project in Manitoba, an outspoken and influential critic of the widespread use of poison to control varmints on federal lands, and the president of the Wildlife Society, all in addition to his teaching responsibilities. Despite this workload, he devoted more time than ever to the activities that would eventually define his legacy: spending time at The Shack, carefully observing the area's natural history, and developing a lyrical writing voice distinct from the dry, authoritative tone of his scientific papers.

The strain of the war years forced Leopold to curtail most of his customary travels. Although he remained involved in the Manitoba waterfowl project, most of his fieldwork took place in Wisconsin, where he was named to the Conservation Commission in 1943. In that capacity, he spent much of the next two years embroiled in debate over a volatile topic familiar to wildlife managers and sportsmen today: the structure of the state's deer season. The herd was overpopulated and starving due to degradation of its habitat. Some factions, including Leopold, recommended the state's first antlerless-only season to reduce herd numbers humanely. Some could not abide the thought of not being able to kill bucks, while others wanted the season closed entirely for the "benefit" of the starving deer. Some sportsmen's groups advocated killing the state's last remaining wolves. Leopold helped engineer compromises that left no one happy, including the deer.

Disillusioned by wildlife politics, Leopold wrote more—and more imaginatively—than ever. Over the years, countless friends and colleagues had encouraged him to publish a collection of his essays. With considerable critical help from his friend, former student, and coworker on the Manitoba waterfowl project Albert Hochbaum, who also provided original illustrations, Leopold revised and polished thirteen of his best short pieces and sent them off to the New York publishing houses Macmillan and Knopf. Both rejected the collection. All outdoor writers who have suffered similar fates should derive some satisfaction from the knowledge that Aldo Leopold had to endure it, too.

Both rejections were polite, but the letter from Knopf editor Clinton Simpson proved useful as well. While expressing admiration for Leopold's prose, he suggested tightening the focus of the essays to a particular place and limiting the subject matter to pure nature observation. We should all enjoy editors with such sound advice.

The end of the war brought a surge of enrollment in Leopold's university classes. He also developed trigeminal neuralgia, a painful disorder with limited and largely ineffective treatment options at the time. These distractions slowed the pace of all his writing. However, in the summer of 1947, he collated and reworked three of his old essays into one, "The Land Ethic," which became one of his most enduring works and the source of one of his most widely cited passages: "Quit thinking about decent land-use as solely an economic problem. Examine each question in terms of what is ethically and esthetically right. A thing is right when it tends to preserve the integrity, stability, and beauty of the biotic community. It is wrong when it tends otherwise."

Leopold also began to restructure his essay collection along the lines Clinton Simpson had suggested. He arranged the essays in three parts: "A Sauk County Almanac," essays about wildlife at The Shack arranged by month; "Sketches Here and There," regionally focused pieces from the Midwest, West, Canada, and Mexico; and "The Upshot," a philosophical conclusion. Leopold called the revised text "Great Possessions" and sent it back to Simpson at Knopf in September 1947.

Later that month, Leopold underwent surgery on his left trigeminal nerve in an attempt to alleviate his progressively debilitating neuralgia. The surgery and convalescence initially went well, though months later he would develop a predictable complication of the procedure: pain and blurred vision in his left eye. Ever the sportsman, Leopold wrote to his son-in-law to complain that "the worst mistake I have made this year was to put off operation until so close to hunting season. I missed opening day on woodcocks."

In November he heard back from Knopf. Simpson expressed enthusiasm for the personal natural history essays but found the rest of the text unpublishable. Discouraged, Leopold turned management of the book project over to his son Luna and went back to his classroom. The manuscript eventually found its way to Oxford University Press, and in April 1948 Leopold received word of its acceptance. Five days later, he died of an apparent heart attack while fighting a brush fire near his rural home.

As an outdoorsman and scientist, Aldo Leopold represents a fairly straightforward subject. His views evolved logically over the course of his life. He left a clear record of his thoughts and achievements, and those accomplishments would have been more than adequate to earn him inclusion among the ranks of conservation's guiding lights.

But as a writer, Leopold was far more complex even in comparison to the larger-than-life personalities who preceded him in the field. Grinnell wrote voluminously in his capacity as editor of *Forest and Stream,* but despite the importance of those writings, hardly anyone today sits down in front of the fireplace to read his work. Roosevelt authored twenty-six books, most of which would largely go unread today if the name *Roosevelt* didn't appear on the cover. In contrast, Leopold's work, especially the small part of it that nearly eluded him at the end, remains current, inspirational, and widely cited. All who care about wildlife know—or think they know—Aldo Leopold.

And with good reason. At his late best, in what eventually became *A Sand County Almanac,* Leopold was simply a terrific writer, with something to say, and say well, to all modern wildlife advocates, whether they hunt as he did or not. The complexity of his legacy arises from that popularity. It's possible to quote something from Leopold to support just about any position on any wildlife question today—and employing the technique of selective citation, plenty of readers have done just that.

But we know this much is true: Aldo Leopold began his life as a sportsman and ended it as one. (Although Leopold stopped hunting big game during the last few years of his life, he remained an avid—and apparently expert—wing-shooter through his last hunting season.) Throughout his career, he actively engaged sportsmen as allies in his efforts to reform state and federal wild-life policies and never hesitated to express his appreciation for their support. He never wavered in his belief that properly conducted hunting was an important component of his environmental philosophy.

As Conrad's Marlowe said of Jim: "He was one of us."

CLOSE CALLS: BIG GAME

On September 17, 1804, Captain William Clark wrote in his journal, "We found the antelope extremely shy and watchful, insomuch as we had been unable to get a shot at them. When at rest, they generally select the most elevated point in the neighborhood, and as they are watchful and extremely quick of sight, and their sense of smelling very acute, it is almost impossible to approach them within gunshot. In sort, they will frequently discover, and flee from, you at a distance of three miles."

As usual, Clark had it right. I too have found the antelope extremely shy and watchful, which explains why I'm plastered to the ground between two clumps of sage holding as still as possible in an attempt to avoid both the cactus thorns studding the dirt and detection by the "extremely quick of sight" animals browsing sixty yards away. And if Clark thought it "impossible to approach within gunshot," he should have tried it with a longbow.

While any of the dozen pronghorns standing in the oblique morning light would make a ready target for a firearm (even Clark's primitive muzzle loader), my own choice of weapon obligates me to cut the range in half, and then nearly in half again. Nonetheless, I have several factors in my favor. A gentle but steady westerly breeze nullifies the keen sense of smell Clark commented upon two centuries earlier, and the rising sun at my back works to the game's optical disadvantage. Furthermore, I'm hunting on the exact same day of the year that Clark was when he made his observations, and mid-September is the peak of the antelope rut. Lust makes males of most species crazy, humans and antelope included.

With all due respect to the outdoor media, no book or video can teach you how to hunt. There is just no substitute for personal time spent in the field, and no substitute for disciplined observation once you're there. Whatever its tactical disadvantages, my bow has allowed me more face time with antelope than most other hunters can imagine, whether they hunt with rifle, camera, or binoculars. Consequently, I know that sometime soon one of the satellite bucks orbiting about the little herd in hope of cutting out a doe will enter the Red Zone: the range at which the dominant herd buck will no longer be able to tolerate his presence. At that point a mighty chase will ensue, and I will take advantage of the buck's distraction to maneuver into position just downwind of his anticipated route of return to his harem.

While the chase is certain given the dynamics of the antelope rut, my proposed strategy for turning it into antelope steaks depends on so many variables that the odds against its success are perhaps ten to one. No matter: I settle back to wait, and to consider once again how improbable the mere opportunity for this encounter would have seemed seventy years ago.

Even now, in a time of relative wildlife abundance, it is sobering to realize how close we came to destroying North America's large mammal population. None of these species ever went the way of the passenger pigeon, although the bison certainly came close, and they were hardly the only species in crisis by the early 1900s. A hundred years later, numbers of almost all of North America's large game animals have rebounded dramatically from their nadirs and many now appear to be approaching or even exceeding historic highs—largely because of policies and support driven and funded by American sportsmen. To appreciate the importance of these developments—as well as to caution ourselves against inappropriate complacency—it will be useful to review the record with regard to several key index species.

Antelope

The American pronghorn is not truly an antelope, but the sole surviving representative of a Pleistocene family of antilocaprid open-plains browsers unique to North America. However, the animal has been called "antelope" for so long—and continues to be so universally—that this conventional if biologically inaccurate term will appear throughout the discussion that follows.

Pre-colonial antelope populations likely numbered between five and ten million animals, distributed north to south between southern Saskatchewan and northern Mexico and east to west from Iowa and Minnesota to the high desert of Oregon and Nevada. Although they never rivaled the bison as a subsistence staple among Native Americans, abundant archeological evidence confirms that Indians did hunt them regularly, often in highly organized fashion. Nonetheless, antelope numbers remained stable prior to our own era of westward expansion.

As Lewis and Clark's *Journals* document, early explorers did kill antelope for the personal use of their meat and hides, but they were not nearly as popular a source of those frontier staples as elk and bison for several reasons. Because of their far greater size, a single bison provided the same nutritional content as nearly twenty antelope, a practical consideration when powder and bullets were scarce. Antelope hides are more fragile and harder to work with than hides from bison and elk. And because of their wariness and keen vision, antelope were particularly difficult to hunt with primitive weapons.

The situation changed during the late 1800s for several reasons. Modern rifles made wary antelope easier to kill. Bison populations were declining rapidly, and commercial markets demanded alternative raw materials to take their place. While antelope meat earned mixed reviews—as it still does today—market demand for it rose steadily. In 1873 Kansas butchers sold antelope meat for 2 cents per pound; by 1879 the price had risen by a factor of five. In addition, tanners had learned to work with antelope hides. In 1873 one Iowa broker sent forty tons of antelope skins to East Coast processors, and fifty-three thousand of them were shipped down the Yellowstone River as late as 1881.

Market pressure wasn't the only force at work against the antelope. "Pot" hunters commonly shot at them from trains and steamboats, wounding or abandoning far more than they salvaged for meat. Encouraged by railroad interests, waves of homesteaders began to arrive on the prairie, creating new subsistence demands for venison. Fences disrupted antelope movement patterns, and domestic livestock competed with them for forage. Millions of acres of antelope habitat were degraded by overgrazing, particularly by sheep, and settlers became progressively less tolerant of wildlife perceived to be competing with their livestock. In 1885 two Colorado ranchers killed over a thousand antelope just to eliminate the animals' grazing impact. And, yes, visiting "sport" hunters, unfettered by seasons, limits, or ethics, killed more than their share.

These pressures were not sustainable. By the early 1900s antelope populations had dropped from millions to less than twenty thousand. While they had once roamed throughout the West wherever they found suitable habitat, they had been eliminated from all states but Montana and Wyoming. Pressured by relentless editorializing from *Forest and Stream,* protests from the Boone and Crockett Club, and lobbying from local sportsmen's clubs around the country, state legislatures belatedly began to act.

Eastern Montana was one of the few areas in the antelope's extensive historic range that still sustained them in any number, though the state's pronghorn population eventually reached a nadir of three thousand after the turn of the century. There were no restrictions at all upon their killing until 1872, when the Territorial Legislature designated the first closed seasons on big game, with unrestricted take allowed during the open season.

In 1895 Montana enacted its first bag limits, restricting each hunter to eight antelope apiece per year—along with eight deer, eight bighorn sheep, eight mountain goats, two moose, and two elk! (It *was* 1895 . . . and it was a start.) Two years later, the state banned the sale of game animals and birds, beginning the elimination of the market trade in meat and hides. In 1910 antelope season closed, not to reopen until 1935, when limited hunting was allowed in a few select Montana counties. Antelope season closed completely again in 1937 and did not reopen until 1943. Legislative restrictions in most western states followed a similar timeline, allowing nearly complete protection for the antelope— at least from law-abiding sportsmen—for decades.

The recovery of Montana's antelope population certainly began with the long ban on all hunting of the species. But it received a tremendous boost in 1946 when state wardens and biologists began to transplant antelope from areas in which they had recovered to parts of their historic range from which they had disappeared. Montana sportsmen volunteered their time and effort to the program, which was largely funded through revenues from the new Pittman-Robertson Act.

As a result of similar efforts in other western states, the country's antelope population has rebounded to somewhere between 500,000 and one million animals. Although this number is well below even the most conservative presettlement estimates, it still represents a major biological success story. The landscape of the western United States has changed so much since the era of Lewis and Clark that restoring original pronghorn numbers throughout their historic range is simply not a realistic goal. Much of that terrain is no longer suitable antelope habitat, for reasons that have nothing to do with hunting. Across much of their current range, antelope are at or near habitat-carrying capacity. The biggest threat to antelope today comes not from regulated hunting, but from habitat degradation by development and intensive grazing practices.

Today, Montana's healthy antelope population allows the state to issue over forty thousand antelope tags annually by special drawing. Rifle hunters are restricted to one of nearly ninety separate districts throughout the state, allowing precise determination of the number of animals that can be taken without biological consequence. Antelope numbers are currently stable or increasing in almost all of those districts.

South of the border, the species has not fared as well: Mexican pronghorns are listed under CITES Appendix 1, and two subspecies (*A. a. peninsularis* and *A. a. sonoriensis*) are listed under our own Endangered Species Act. Mexican pronghorns probably number fewer than a thousand animals. The species' experience in this neighboring nation is illustrative: It is no accident that antelope are endangered in a country where game laws, habitat protection, and game law enforcement are lax while they are thriving just across the border, where sportsmen have served as their consistent advocates for the last century.

Elk

The first mention of elk in the Corps of Discovery's records came on July 14, 1804, when Clark spotted some on a sandbar in what is now Nebraska (where there were no elk at all when I was born). He put ashore and tried to kill one, but missed. He made no comment on the animals' appearance other than to identify them as elk, suggesting familiarity with the species even though Clark had not previously ventured beyond the Mississippi.

The *Journals* contain numerous references to elk as the expedition crossed the plains to the Rockies. In fact, elk were critical to the expedition's success. During the long layover at Fort Clatsop on the Pacific during the winter of 1804–5, elk meat supplied the bulk of their nutrition. Sergeant Gass reported that the expedition's hunters killed 131 from December through March; the expedition might well have died of starvation without them. (C. Hart Merriam would later describe this coastal Pacific Northwest elk as a new species and name it *Cervus roosevelti* in honor of the Boone and Crockett Club's co-founder.) As in the case of the antelope and the bison, the wapiti's abundance was not destined to survive the century.

At the time of first European contact, one did not have to travel to the Pacific to find elk. The eastern subspecies thrived in portions of the original thirteen colonies as far eastward as Pennsylvania. Largely due to subsistence hunting pressure and habitat destruction, this elk population had already started to decline by the time of the Revolution. The last pure eastern elk was killed in Pennsylvania in 1877.

During the nineteenth-century era of westward expansion, the plains elk population described by Lewis and Clark declined precipitously due to a number of by now familiar factors, principally unregulated subsistence hunting by settlers and commercial hunting for hides and horns. Elk were rapidly eliminated from the midwestern portion of their range; the last native elk in Wisconsin was killed in 1866. Matters grew worse when a fraternal group called the Jolly Corkers changed their name to the Elks in 1868. When they adopted the elk's unique "ivory" tooth as their emblem, commercial demand increased even further.

Later, unregulated sport hunters from the East Coast and especially Europe contributed significantly to the elk's decline. While the numbers they killed didn't approach those accounted for by market hunters, visiting "sportsmen" probably impacted elk more than any other western big game species for two reasons. First, elk antlers make a particularly majestic trophy. (Mounted bison heads didn't become popular until the species' impending near-extinction made them collectors' items in the 1890s.) Second, by the time the railroads offered recreational hunters ready access to the West, elk were one of the few remaining trophy animals that remained. Of course, these developments only emphasized the need for appropriate hunting regulations and the development of meaningful outdoor ethics—challenges to which American sportsmen eventually rose.

Estimates of North American elk populations prior to European settlement range from two to ten million. By the beginning of the twentieth century, that number, whatever it actually was, had fallen to around fifty thousand. The reduction in the species' range was as dramatic as its decline in numbers. Not only were wild, free-ranging elk gone east of the Mississippi, they had also vanished from the open plains where Lewis and Clark had described them in such abundance.

The same social and political pressures—largely driven by sportsmen—that snatched the pronghorn back from the brink also came into play on behalf of the elk. Again, Montana's experience provides an appropriate model, especially since the majority of the nation's surviving elk lay within its borders. As with antelope, the first legal hunting seasons were created in 1872, the first annual limit (two) in 1895. The state's 1897 ban on the sale of game birds and animals spelled the beginning of the end for the market trade. The annual limit on elk was reduced to one in 1910, and the same year, the state began to reintroduce elk to parts of their historic range from which they had been eliminated. The first transplant involved moving elk from Yellowstone National Park to Fleecer Mountain, near Butte. The actual work was done by state wardens and sportsmen volunteering their time. In fact, hunters paid the expenses for the first transplant out of their own pockets.

At the time, none of these measures received much support from state legislators, who faced pressure from farm and ranch interests to limit elk numbers because of crop damage and grazing competition with domestic livestock, just as they do today. Lobbying by sportsmen's groups—local, state, and national—was instrumental in the passage of basic regulations to protect elk populations as they recovered.

By the Second World War, habitat concerns had replaced market hunting as the principal threat to game populations, including elk. Human encroachment (which elk tolerate poorly), overgrazing, excess logging, and suppression of natural fires all represented threats to elk as they began to repopulate their historic ranges. Pittman-Robertson funds became vital in efforts to secure critical habitat, especially on important winter range.

Elk numbers responded to similar measures around the country, eventually rising from a low of several thousand to an estimated eight hundred thousand, and are approaching historic highs (and straining habitat-carrying capacity) in some western states today. The restoration of the species to its original range may be as gratifying as its overall population increase. Self-sustaining elk herds are now thriving in many of the eastern and midwestern states from which they had been entirely extirpated early in the twentieth century, including Pennsylvania, Kentucky, and Nebraska, where Lewis and Clark first met them two centuries earlier. Much credit for these developments goes to the hunter-driven Rocky Mountain Elk Foundation.

Bison

We have already examined the precipitous collapse of North American bison populations in the late 1800s and the role sportsmen like George Grinnell and John Lacey played in establishing Yellowstone as a haven for some of the last survivors. At the beginning of the next century, sportsmen were also key players in a sequence of events vital to the bison's ultimate survival as a species.

At the time, the population of bison in the public domain was limited to the two-dozen head in Yellowstone that authorities had managed to save from poachers and a few individual specimens in the National Zoological Park in Washington. Even the optimistic Grinnell privately expressed doubts that the meager Yellowstone population could be saved. The remainder of the nation's inventory was limited to two small, confined herds in Texas and Montana, privately maintained through a combination of altruism and an eye to profit from a vanishing breed.

The larger of the two, the Montana herd, derived largely from a group of eight orphaned calves that had followed a Pend d'Oreille Indian named Samuel Walking Coyote home to the Flathead Valley after a buffalo hunt just south of the Canadian border thirty years earlier. Two locals of mixed Indian, French-Canadian, and Mexican ancestry, Charles Allard and Michael Pablo, recognized the potential value of the bison as the great herds approached extinction on the plains, and they purchased Walking Coyote's stock.

Supplemented by additional breeding stock obtained from hide-hunter-turned-Yellowstone-warden Charles "Buffalo" Jones, the Pablo-Allard herd grew to three hundred head in Montana's Flathead Valley. Meanwhile, a former Texas Ranger named Charles Goodnight preserved a small herd on his beef ranch in the Texas panhandle with vague aims of breeding them into "cattalo." The future of the species rested precariously upon these small, isolated populations of bison.

Given the severely limited gene pool of the remaining Yellowstone herd and the at least partially commercial motives of Allard, Pablo, and Goodnight, the bison's chance of survival seemed guarded at best without some form of guidance to oversee its future. That arrived just in time, with the formation of the American Bison Society in 1905. Sportsmen were crucial to the society's founding. Its president was Dr. William Hornaday—eccentric, zoologist, scientific innovator, and hunter. Theodore Roosevelt became honorary president.

While Roosevelt needs no further introduction, Hornaday is a new entry in our cast of characters. Born in Indiana in 1854, he attended college in Iowa before going to work for Ward's National Science Foundation in 1873. For several years he made extensive collecting trips throughout the Caribbean, South America, and Southeast Asia—hunting with scientific justification just as Lewis and Clark had done and Roosevelt himself would do when he left the presidency and headed to Africa to take hundreds of specimens for the American Museum of Natural History.

After his appointment as chief taxidermist of the National Museum (the Smithsonian) in 1882, he led an 1886 expedition west to obtain bison specimens. In a letter back to the Smithsonian at its conclusion, he wrote:

> The total number of buffalos killed on the Expedition, including last spring's work, was 25. I consider that we have been extremely lucky in finding a sufficient number of buffalo where it was supposed by people generally that none existed. Our "outfit" has been pronounced by old buffalo hunters "The luckiest outfit that ever hunted buffalo in Montana" and the opinion is quite generally held that our "haul" of specimens could not be equaled again in Montana by anybody . . . We killed very nearly all we saw and I am confident that there are not thirty-head remaining in Montana all told.

The irony of killing an estimated half of Montana Territory's remaining buffalo in the name of science appears to have been utterly lost upon Hornaday at the time, establishing that his concept of outdoor ethics, like that of so many other American outdoorsmen, was still very much a work in progress. His later writings suggest that his subsequent dedication to the bison's cause reflected an attempt at atonement.

The society's first order of business was to create dedicated living space for the country's last surviving bison. It successfully promoted a congressional bill authorizing the creation of the National Bison Range at the southern end of Flathead Valley, where Walking Coyote's orphaned calves had grown into the Allard-Pablo herd. Roosevelt signed the bill into law in 1909. By then, Allard was dead and Pablo had tired of tending bison. Our Congress waffled when he tried to sell his herd to the government, but Canada's did not. By the time our country had a Bison Range, most of the animals that should have populated it were either in Canada or on their way. The Bison Society undertook the private responsibility of raising the money needed to buy back breeding stock.

Over the course of the next several years, the society also raised the funds needed to restock the Wichita Forest Reserve (Roosevelt's first game reserve, created in 1907) with excess bison from New York City's zoos and introduce fresh genetics from Goodnight's Texas herd. The society also funded successful bison transplantation to Fort Niobrara, in Nebraska, and Wind Cave National Park, in South Dakota.

Questions and controversies about the ultimate future of wild bison persist to this day. However those issues play out, they would be irrelevant if the species had not survived the first decades of the twentieth century. Without active, foresighted intervention by sportsmen-conservationists, that no doubt would have been the case.

Grizzly Bear

No animal in North America has generated more fear, awe, legend, and controversy than the grizzly. The big bears provide an interesting contrast to the species just reviewed. The grizzly is more averse to human presence than any other large mammal on the continent and is still listed under the Endangered Species Act (ESA) in the Lower 48 (although thanks to successful recovery efforts, this should be about to change). And while sportsmen played a well-defined role in the restoration of pronghorn, elk, and other ungulate populations, their record of advocacy for the grizzly is less consistent, reflecting discomfort with large predators on behalf of both sportsmen and society at large.

At the time of European settlement, an estimated 50,000 to 100,000 grizzlies roamed what is now the continental United States, from the Great Plains to the Pacific Ocean. Substantially more inhabited western Canada and Alaska. Grizzlies originally populated the New World by migrating eastward across the Bering Sea land bridge, and large numbers of the same ursine species also lived in northern Eurasia, as they do today.

Although the bears were alien to settled areas along the eastern seaboard, eighteenth-century Americans knew something of their existence through the writings of early Canadian explorers such as Alexander Mackenzie. Those reports were sketchy at best, and the first accurate descriptions of the bear came, not surprisingly, from Lewis and Clark. They encountered the animal regularly on their way across the plains, referring to it variously as the "white bear," "white or grey bear," "yellow bear," "brown bear," and finally "Brown or Grisley" (Clark) and "brown grizzly" (Lewis). Their records leave no doubt about its abundance or its ferocity when wounded.

Native Americans did hunt grizzlies, but usually for ritualistic or ceremonial purposes that had minimal if any biological impact upon bear numbers. Commercial harvest for the fur trade began to affect bear populations in the early 1800s. Hudson's Bay Company records indicate that between 1827 and 1859, nearly four thousand grizzly hides were processed from the North Cascades alone. But the bear's critical decline didn't begin until the period of intense western expansion during the second half of the century, when grizzlies faced accelerated habitat loss, unregulated sport hunting, competition with livestock for living space, and ever-increasing numbers of people, with whom they had always coexisted uneasily at best.

For decades the bears were shot on sight, usually because of a real or perceived threat to the safety of humans or livestock. By 1890 the bears had been extirpated from the eastern portion of their historic range, from Texas north across the plains to the Dakotas. The last California grizzly was killed in 1924, eliminating the subspecies *Ursus arctos californicus*. The bear was gone from Oregon by 1933, from the Desert Southwest a few years later. Of thirty-seven distinct grizzly populations recognized in the Lower 48 in 1922, thirty-one had been completely extirpated by 1975. While isolated populations endured in remote portions of the northern Rockies near Glacier and Yellowstone National Parks, by the 1950s the grizzly had been eliminated from 98 percent of its historic range in the contiguous states.

As with antelope, elk, and bison, Montana remained one of the last strongholds of the grizzly as its numbers relentlessly declined elsewhere, so the state's legislative experience again proves illustrative. While basic regulatory restrictions were being enacted for ungulate game species as early as 1872, grizzlies received no protection at all from the state until fifty years later, when they were finally classified as game animals in 1922. Montana then held regulated grizzly bear seasons until the species' listing by the Endangered Species Act. Between 1950 and 1970, hunters killed an average of thirty-seven Montana grizzlies annually.

When the U.S. Fish and Wildlife Service (USFWS) listed the Lower 48 grizzly population as threatened according to ESA criteria in 1975, state regulations regarding the bears became irrelevant outside of Alaska. This ruling affected five populations of grizzlies, the large majority in the Yellowstone area (9,200 square miles in Wyoming, Montana, and Idaho) and the Northern Continental Divide Ecosystem (9,600 square miles in Montana). Much smaller populations of bears remained in Washington's North Cascades, the Selkirk Mountains of Washington and Idaho, and the Cabinet-Yaak area of Montana and Idaho.

In 2007 the Fish and Wildlife Service announced that the Yellowstone grizzly population (numerically the largest of the five) had recovered and no longer met ESA criteria as endangered or threatened. While attaining this goal represents another obvious biological success story, it also begs an important question: *Now what?* Delisting potentially means resumption of bear management by the states, including the possibility of bear hunting seasons, if wildlife authorities in Montana, Wyoming, and Idaho can produce management plans acceptable to the USFWS. Given recent experience following the delisting of the timber wolf in the same tristate area and western states' traditional antipathy toward large predators, that's unlikely to be as easy as it sounds. The history of wolf recovery and delisting also foretells expensive and protracted rounds of litigation.

The bears' eventual legal status and the role sportsmen will play in determining it remain uncertain. This represents a remarkable opportunity for hunting and non-hunting wildlife advocates to work together for the good of all involved, including the bears, although given the degree of emotionalism regarding large predators on both sides, it's difficult to be optimistic.

The gratifying recovery of the Yellowstone grizzly population confirms the wisdom of the 1975 listing and the closed hunting seasons it entailed. But the ecological principles articulated by Aldo Leopold hold that once a depressed wildlife population has recovered above a certain critical level (in this instance, the recovery criteria originally established by the USFWS), the properly regulated removal of some individuals will have no overall impact upon the population as a whole. In sum, carefully regulated grizzly bear hunting may soon be both legally and biologically feasible.

Of course, many non- and anti-hunting members of the organized grizzly bear advocacy community find that idea illogical if not downright abhorrent. (In fact, the organized grizzly bear advocacy community consists almost entirely of non- and anti-hunters—a discredit to hunters who choose not to care and a reminder of what will happen when they don't.) How could hunting grizzlies possibly benefit the species?

The answers are both biological and social. The Greater Yellowstone Ecosystem can only hold so many grizzlies—its carrying capacity. Natural forces will attempt to limit the bear population to that level in a number of ways. Mature boars will kill more cubs. Displaced subadults will disperse to areas more densely populated by humans, increasing the number of adverse encounters between people and grizzlies, a situation that never benefits large predators. Controlled hunting may be a preferred alternative.

Socially, one must remember that the ultimate threat to grizzlies comes not from bullets but from development. Grizzlies have more demanding habitat requirements than any other large mammal on the continent, and what they require most is large tracts of wild space—and this at a time when such spaces face ever-increasing pressure from all the usual suspects ranging from mining and energy interests to naive newcomers to the West determined to build trophy houses in the wrong places. In the battles such conflicts always engender, wildlife needs all the supporters it can muster. The more people who have a vested interest in grizzlies, the better off the bears will be. Sportsmen have consistently shown—consider the case of North American waterfowl, for example—that when it is in their interest to do so, they can mobilize more financial and political resources on behalf of wildlife than any other segment of society. It worked for ducks, and there's no reason why it can't work for bears.

In fact, it already has, in the true last bastion of the grizzly. Alaska's population of brown/grizzly bears (the two are the same species, *Ursus arctos*) dwarfs that of the Lower 48. Extensively studied and carefully managed (with some recent exceptions), Alaska's grizzly population has been stable for decades at or near historic highs. Credit for some of that security falls simply to terrain: Most Alaska grizzlies live in largely inaccessible places. But Alaska is growing just like the Mountain West, if not in terms of absolute human numbers, certainly in terms of humans' ability to reach the more remote corners of the North.

However, even as opportunities for encounters between bears and humans escalated, Alaska's grizzly population did not suffer the same fate as, say, California's, largely because the state recognized the bears' value as game animals and treated them accordingly—originally at the urging of Alaska's old-time brown bear guides.

The decade following the Second World War saw a dramatic decrease in the most famous brown bear population in the world, Kodiak Island's. The pressure arose from two sources. The general postwar boom in outdoor recreation brought a sharp increase in sport hunting for the island's famous bears even though bear hunting was largely unregulated at the time. Furthermore, an ill-advised attempt to develop commercial cattle ranching on Kodiak led to inevitable encounters between bears and beef. Ranchers countered the threat to their stock by killing bears on sight, including aerial gunning that went on for years with at least the tacit approval of state authorities.

The renowned bear guiding team of Bill Pinnell and Morris Talifson (still known up North simply as "P&T") was among the first to identify declining bear numbers and propose concrete remedies. In 1957 they successfully lobbied for regulations prohibiting killing cubs or females accompanied by cubs on Kodiak, common sense restrictions that eventually became established wildlife law throughout the state.

In 1963 cattlemen killed an estimated thirty-five to forty-five brown bears on Kodiak, many from a specially outfitted Piper aircraft. Pinnell and Talifson had had enough. They organized other guides in protest, and the offending aircraft was grounded. Over the next several years, they continued to fight for increasing restrictions on seasons and bag limits and against unethical "bandit" guides, and because of their stature in the Alaska outdoor community, they won most of those battles. As Pinnell later recalled: "There's no one in this state who has done more for the welfare of our game than Morris and I have. We battled the cattlemen, fought for shorter seasons, stricter regulations, and better enforcement. We accomplished the sow with cub law, and greatly influenced the one bear per four years bag limit, but some people still don't see that."

Again, it's easy to invoke self-interest: A lot of hunters will pay a lot of money to hunt Alaska grizzlies. So what? Because of that self-interest, Alaska still has its bears.

This brief survey may seem artificially skewed toward western game species. But the Mountain West is home to a far greater variety of large mammals than any other part of the country outside Alaska. From open prairies to alpine peaks, it offers more choices of habitat niches to fill. It made a logical stopping point for the great body of North American mammals that arrived from Eurasia by the Bering Sea land bridge, including wild sheep, moose, elk, wolves, and grizzlies. And in important respects, western species provide more appropriate models for the study of all that can happen when interactions between humans and game animals go wrong.

The only large wild mammals widely distributed throughout all thirteen original colonies were the black bear, cougar, and white-tailed deer, of which the latter was by far the most numerous and important to American settlers. While the eastern black bear and cougar suffered many of the same problems faced by elk, bison, and other western species, the whitetail, a remarkably adaptive animal, eventually demonstrated the ability to prosper in proximity to human development. The same agricultural practices that threatened critical habitat for elk and antelope merely provided important additional food sources for the whitetail. The whitetail has little difficulty utilizing small patches of edge habitat as security cover, as residents of many eastern suburbs realize all too well today.

In short, the whitetail is a survivor, the converse of the doomed passenger pigeon. With more restrictive habitat requirements, less efficient reproductive capacity, and intrinsically less tolerance for human presence, western species like the antelope, elk, and grizzly require far more enlightened human management.

While whitetail numbers did indeed drop to worrisome levels throughout much of their range by the early twentieth century, they enjoy an innate capacity for recovery that other big game animal species do not. There would likely be whitetails in North America no matter what we did; the same cannot be said for any other native large mammal with the possible exception of the coyote.

Back in the sagebrush, one of the satellite bucks is making his move, trying to act casual as he closes the gap toward the indifferent does by an indirect route, and pretending to nibble at the browse as he slowly works closer beneath the herd buck's steady gaze. Finally he crosses an invisible line. The herd buck lowers his head and the chase is on.

My ringside seat at the show allows an opportunity to observe pure Darwinian theory in action. Splendidly adapted to their open savannah habitat, the pronghorn only has to do two things well: see and run. And does it ever; the pronghorn's vision is legendary, and it is the second-fastest land animal in the world, capable of speeds exceeded only by the cheetah. But the cat is a sprinter that only requires short bursts of speed over the distances necessary to catch its prey—the true antelope of southern Africa. Our pronghorn, on the other hand, can add endurance to the equation, cruising at speeds of fifty miles per hour for miles. The wild chase I'm witnessing now serves but one evolutionary purpose: to ensure that next year's fawns hit the ground carrying the swiftest genetics possible.

With the two bucks suddenly out of sight beyond a hill over a mile distant, I take advantage of a fold in the terrain that allows me to crawl undetected into a position near the herd buck's likeliest return route. This is all a crapshoot, of course, but ten minutes later a pale figure appears in the sage several hundred yards away, inbound toward the does at a brisk walk. After some last-minute guesswork, I identify a dense clump of sage that will provide some cover and scoot toward it on my belly. Then I nock an arrow, rise to one knee, and wait.

Ten minutes later I'm standing over the fallen buck. Cruel? Hardly, not when one considers the likely alternatives: starving during the winter or dying of disease, becoming fodder for a cast of scavengers ranging from magpies to golden eagles, or getting dragged down and torn apart by coyotes. The buck was fated to wind up as someone's dinner from the start; I just happened to be the predator in the right place at the right time. And without the efforts of others like me, this fallen buck would not be here today, alive or dead. Neither would the smaller buck he chased over the hill to pass along his genes another time, or the dozen does that raced over the hill unharmed when I rose from my ambush. I can live with the hint of regret the dead animal evokes. We have done our part.

Close Calls: Beyond Big Game

One overcast day last winter, I sat in a skiff with a shotgun in my lap watching large flocks of diving ducks trade up and down the Columbia River. The birds were all well beyond the margins of our decoy spread, but the bounty was fascinating just from an observer's perspective: goldeneyes, redheads, scaup, and—most exciting of all—canvasbacks. I'd stopped shooting cans when their population crashed years earlier, but now their numbers were doing so well across the continent that Washington State's regulations allowed hunters two per day for the first time in memory. I wasn't just duck hunting—I was watching another wildlife success story play out before my eyes.

In 1897 a onetime market hunter named Forest McNeir and a hunting companion set out on a lake in coastal Texas where McNeir ran a hunting camp for a wealthy Galveston businessman. As McNeir later wrote:

It began to get rough out in the middle, and they [canvasbacks] took a notion they wanted to be up in the east end of the lake around the small islands. To get there, they had to pass our end of the island. We didn't shoot into the front end of the big bunches as they dived for our decoys, but we tore into the back end, and shot all the scattering ducks that came along. I never got my pump gun fully loaded after the first round. The ducks came so thick and fast that a lot of them got by us while we were reloading. Our shells lasted forty-five minutes. When we quit shooting, all the rushes around our skiff had shed their ice and were standing up from the heat of those 300 rounds of black powder. We picked up 192 fat canvasbacks, worth big money on the New York market for the Christmas holidays.

This simple description of less than an hour's events over a century ago emphasizes two important points about canvasback ducks: They were historically present in abundance, and their market value nearly did them in.

The can has always enjoyed special esteem among North American waterfowl. It is the largest of our divers, and the drake's russet head and distinctive sloping facial profile make it a particularly attractive bird. The canvasback is the fastest duck on the continent. It shares its specific name, *valiseneria,* with the generic name of the wild celery upon which it preferentially feeds, demonstrating that even early biologists recognized the importance of this specific food source to the well-being of the species.

The canvasback's vegetarian diet, rare among diving ducks, makes it the most savory of our waterfowl on the table. Roasted canvasback was a high-end restaurant staple at the end of the last century. Vintage menus suggest that it was the only wild duck species that patrons routinely asked for by name—in the best restaurants there were simply canvasbacks and all the rest. Those same menus also reflect trends in the birds' numbers. In 1860, when they were still plentiful, canvasback dinners averaged $20 in modern currency. By 1910, they were scarce enough to command a $100 price tag. With money like that at stake, market hunters were only too happy to keep making them scarcer.

Careful monitoring by the U.S. Fish and Wildlife Service (USFWS) provided highly accurate records of waterfowl population numbers throughout the last half of the twentieth century, the most accurate of any such numbers discussed in this book. In response to habitat improvement and regulatory reforms, North American duck populations generally increased during the 1950s and '60s, but canvasback numbers lagged behind the trend. By 1972 they had fallen so drastically that the USFWS closed the season on canvasbacks completely.

What was wrong with the "king of ducks?" My own brief literature search revealed the following hypotheses: poisoning by lead shot, a decline in wild celery due to pollution, alterations in winter habitat by hurricanes, pesticides, drought, loss of breeding habitat to agriculture, spring egg harvest by Alaska Natives, parasites, increased nesting predation by raccoons (whose numbers were increasing on the Canadian prairies because of changing agricultural practices), illegal sport hunting in violation of closed seasons, and degradation of freshwater habitat by invasive carp species. The abundance of theories simply confirms that no one knows the answer.

Most of these considerations, however, would have applied to waterfowl across the board, and the fact that canvasbacks were in trouble while populations of other ducks were stable or increasing suggests vulnerabilities unique to the species. Among other factors, canvasbacks simply have more rigid habitat requirements than most waterfowl. They need to breed on big water (making them more vulnerable to drought), and they have relatively fixed dietary requirements (making them vulnerable to the collapse of a single food source, like wild celery). The less flexibility a species enjoys, the more vulnerable it becomes to environmental stress of any kind.

Some variation on these themes likely spelled the end of the Labrador duck, but events took a different turn for the canvasback. By the 1990s the canvasback population had risen above the North American Waterfowl Management Plan's target of 540,000, and hunters were allowed to shoot one canvasback per day in most parts of the country. Since the exact cause of the species' original decline remains uncertain, it's hard to know what was responsible for its recovery. However, habitat enhancement on summer breeding grounds and the prompt institution of a closed season years earlier almost certainly played a part. Neither would have been possible without sportsmen, who funded habitat projects both directly and indirectly and drove home the original legislation that made prompt and effective management of waterfowl seasons possible.

Even though we may never be certain exactly what happened and why, the end result was undeniably good for the canvasbacks. From a modern continental population nadir of less than 300,000 in the 1980s, canvasback numbers climbed to 400,000 in the year 2000 and then to 850,000 in 2007, at which point the USFWS raised the daily limit to two cans a day in many areas. It couldn't have happened to a nicer duck.

The successful recovery of the canvasback illustrates important points. While public opinion instinctively focuses upon dramatic, sexy animals like grizzlies and wolves, species a bit farther down the food chain are just as important to wild ecosystems and may provide even more accurate indicators of their overall health. And sportsmen were just as important in the historic record of their recovery as they were in the cases of bison and elk, as demonstrated by the following examples.

RED DRUM

Sometime in the late 1970s New Orleans chef Paul Prudhomme retired to the kitchen in his French Quarter restaurant K-Paul's, tinkered with an incendiary mixture of seasonings and a red-hot skillet, and invented blackened redfish. The dish became an overnight sensation all across the country. Regional cuisine was rapidly growing popular as Americans belatedly began to realize that there can be more to dinner than meat and potatoes. Health-conscious diners were (rightly or not) eager for alternatives to red meat. And

Prudhomme's ebullient personality proved ideally suited to two other recent social phenomena: the celebrity chef and the television cooking show.

But why redfish? Prior to their blackening, sophisticated diners had never paid much attention to red drum on the table. The Gulf Coast produces a number of fish that make better eating, and drum were widely regarded as a culinary trash fish. Furthermore, as anyone who has prepared blackened redfish knows, the spices make the fish beneath them virtually unidentifiable anyway. Prudhomme may have chosen the redfish because its firm flesh holds up well in all that scorching heat, but more likely he picked it simply because it was cheap and locally abundant.

But not for long. Some fish populations resist commercial pressure because they are difficult to catch in quantity or live a long way from potential markets, but in the case of the redfish, the stability of their numbers largely reflected lack of demand. Prudhomme's Magic Blackened Redfish Spice took care of that. Recreational anglers usually pursue redfish in their shallow inshore habitat. Those five- to ten-pound reds are fun to catch on light tackle, but they're almost always sexually immature fish. As they age and grow they move offshore, where big breeding reds form huge surface schools prior to spawning. Aided by spotter planes, commercial netters can haul in a lot of prime breeders in a hurry, and when the market told them it was suddenly worthwhile to do so, they did.

Redfish populations plummeted around the Gulf. A small group of concerned recreational anglers in Texas founded the Coastal Conservation Association (CCA) to try to halt the depletion of local redfish stocks. From that humble beginning, the CCA's "Save the Redfish" campaign spread around the Gulf; by 1985 chapters had formed from Texas to Florida. Operating at both the state and national level, over the course of the next decade the CCA helped draft and support legislation that obtained game fish status for previously unprotected redfish in other states, outlawed gill nets in Texas, halted the commercial harvest of adult redfish throughout the Gulf, prohibited the sale of wild redfish in Texas, won approval for saltwater recreational fishing stamps in a number of states to provide a source of funding for enforcement and research, and successfully backed a Florida state constitutional amendment limiting marine netting.

Although it arose as a regional organization focused upon the conservation of redfish, the CCA has grown with time. By the early 1990s its fifteen coastal state chapters extended north along the Atlantic seaboard to New England. They have now successfully backed legislation targeting the conservation of billfish, sea trout, tarpon, cobia, mackerel, and other marine species—not to mention entire ecosystems.

Recent events in Texas illustrate the last point. Even after the redfish nets were gone, inshore commercial shrimp fishermen were stressing the coastal ecosystem through their incidental bycatch of croaker, sand trout, and anchovies—species of little direct importance to recreational anglers, but critical to the base of the food chain that supports everything from invertebrates to redfish and sea trout. Sensitive to the needs of commercial fishermen who depended on the shrimp fishery for their livelihood, the Texas legislature authorized a voluntary buyout program for the fixed number of existing commercial shrimp licenses. Funding for the buyouts originally depended on private sources and a surcharge on commercial licenses, but in 2000 the Texas Parks and Wildlife Commission approved a $3 surcharge on the saltwater fishing stamps required of the state's coastal sport anglers, most of them targeting redfish.

Funds derived from this surcharge eventually allowed the state to buy back 1,800 commercial shrimp licenses. Bay shrimping efforts decreased by over 90 percent; counts of forage fish doubled. "Our goal was to return bay shrimping efforts to the levels of the 1970s and we've done that," Coastal Fisheries Division director Larry McKinney reported in 2007. "Our red drum and trout fisheries are in their best condition in thirty years, with populations increasing." Of course, with balance restored to the ecosystem, countless other species benefited too, from crustaceans to wading birds.

Paul Prudhomme eventually stopped serving redfish in his restaurant. I do not know whether that decision reflects remorse or a principled culinary decision not to substitute inferior fish-farm reds for the real, wild thing. I do know that every time a recreational angler catches a redfish, he or she should take time to thank the people who made it possible.

AMERICAN ALLIGATOR

Here are three interesting points on the timeline of the American alligator, all within a tiny fragment of the species' 200-million-year lifespan on Earth:

In 1770 naturalist William Bartram made the following observation while visiting Florida's Saint Johns River: "Alligators are in such numbers and so close together from shore to shore that it would have been easy to have walked across on their heads had the animals been harmless."

In 1958 I saw my first alligator. Although my family lived in upstate New York at the time, we traveled regularly to Florida to fish. Over the preceding five years, I had spent many days with my father in prime alligator habitat without ever seeing one. Then one day we rounded a bend in our canoe and watched a six-foot gator slide off the bank and glide underneath us. My father was clearly excited. Although he was an experienced outdoorsman, this was his first wild gator sighting as well as mine. That was the only alligator we ever saw while fishing together in Florida.

In 2000 I was back in Florida for the first time in decades, not counting stops in the Miami airport en route to other places. One of the friends we were visiting invited us to take a ride in his airboat up the same Saint Johns that Bartram described. When I asked if we might see an alligator, he just smiled. I soon learned why. After a short run in his boat, we entered an undeveloped stretch of wild Florida. Alligators waited for us at every turn: dozens around the course of each bend, hundreds over the course of the evening.

There you have a familiar sequence: abundance, decimation, recovery. Alligators are not always thought of as a game species, but I have hunted them with my bow and enjoyed enough success to confirm the most admiring opinions of gator meat on the table. Reviewing the turbulent course of their population collapse and subsequent rebound provides an illustrative example of the perils and potentials facing huntable wildlife in America. Indeed, it would be hard to identify another species that matched the extent of the alligator's collapse or the success of its eventual recovery.

Of the world's twenty-three crocodilian species, only two are true alligators, ours and a smaller Chinese resident of the Yangtze Basin. Best-guess estimates place America's pre-colonial alligator population around one million. Native Americans killed some gators for meat, with their usual minimal impact on their numbers. While I find alligator meat delicious, most early colonists didn't care much for it, and gators didn't face significant subsistence hunting pressure from them either.

But meat isn't the sole potentially valuable part of an alligator. No doubt the alligator would have been better off without its black, glossy hide, which tans into a distinctively beautiful leather. During the 1800s alligator hides sold for $7 apiece in Miami, the equivalent of several weeks' wages for a laborer. Alligator leather became a high-fashion commodity during the early 1900s, when tens of thousands of alligators per year were turned into boots, belts, handbags, and briefcases. Alligator hide was worth a lot of money, and it still is. I just googled a watch from Neiman-Marcus featuring a black alligator band and a price tag over $40,000.

After decades of totally unregulated commercial hide hunting and trapping, alligator populations had begun to decline rapidly by the time of the Second World War. In 1943 Florida established a four-foot minimum size limit, the first attempt to restrict the gator harvest in any way. All Florida alligator hunting became illegal in 1962.

Protected Florida alligators faced the same problem protected Yellowstone elk and bison faced in the late 1800s: inadequate law enforcement. Alligators inhabited remote, nearly inaccessible habitat where they were hunted by skilled local poachers who knew the terrain better than the game wardens did. As alligator numbers continued to drop, it became apparent that the enforcement battle would not be won in the swamps.

In 1967 the alligator was placed on the first federal Endangered Species List, a precursor to the Endangered Species Act (ESA) of 1973. That was little more than a gesture, as there were no real provisions for enforcement. Enter an old friend—the Lacey Act. A 1970 amendment to the original statute made the interstate transport of alligator hides illegal, and the commercial market finally began to dry up. Today, many environmentalists cite the 1973 ESA as the legislation that made gator hunting illegal and saved the species. In fact, Florida law had granted complete protection to the alligator for over a decade by that time, and it was the Lacey Act that made possible the crucial intervention: disruption of the commercial market in alligator hides.

No matter who or what properly gets credit, the alligator certainly made a prompt and dramatic comeback. It was delisted under the ESA in 1987 and remains classified as threatened only because of its physical resemblance to the still-endangered American crocodile. Florida now conducts tightly regulated alligator hunting. Interestingly, while sportsmen are issued tags through a lottery system that allows them to take some eight thousand alligators per year, twice that number of "problem alligators" are killed annually by wildlife agents and contract hunters as more and more Floridians wake up to find alligators in their swimming pools.

What role did sportsmen play in this success story? Not much . . . at first glance. Despite the quality of their meat, alligators have never aroused wide enthusiasm in traditional hunting circles. They don't appear regularly on the cover of outdoor magazines, and no sportsman-driven organizations lobby specifically on their behalf as they do for elk, wild sheep, pheasant, quail, wild turkey, and many other familiar game species. Sportsmen were no more vociferous in their defense of the alligator than non-hunting conservationists of many different backgrounds.

However, this does not mean that sportsmen were anything less than instrumental in the alligator's recovery. It was the Lacey

Act, and not the ESA, that provided the original legal basis for the disruption of the commercial trade in alligator hides, and sportsmen were responsible for that legislation. Furthermore, necessary law enforcement at the state level depended heavily on funding from the Pittman-Robertson Act. A duck hunter buys a shotgun in Minnesota; game wardens bust an alligator poacher in Florida. That really is the way it works.

The problem with success is that it breeds complacency, and that is certainly not the intent of the last two chapters. If the history of two centuries' worth of wildlife management and mismanagement prove anything, it's that wildlife advocates can never afford to underestimate the threats posed by irresponsible development, habitat degradation, and commercial exploitation of wild resources. But let's be honest: It's nice to hear some good news on the environmental front for a change. Furthermore, analyzing past success is just as crucial to the future as analyzing past failure. Stories like these not only show that it can be done, they show how to do it.

While I think I have made a good case for the role sportsmen played in restoring threatened populations of these representative species, I cannot pretend that they were blameless in their near demise. USFWS agents monitoring hunting activities at a popular waterfowl area one year showed that a disturbing 40 percent of the hunting parties under observation shot at canvasbacks when the season was completely closed to their taking. There is no way to know whether the shooting represented inability to identify canvasbacks on the wing, ignorance of widely publicized regulations, or deliberate attempts to kill a protected species. From a practical standpoint, it doesn't matter.

And the naive assumption that fish take by recreational anglers is always inconsequential in comparison to the commercial harvest no longer holds true for some species, including redfish. In 2005 recreational anglers harvested just under 500,000 redfish totaling 1.54 million pounds. The previous year's commercial harvest was just 54,700 pounds. The issue isn't lack of regulation in the recreational fishery. Thanks to state legislation sponsored by the CCA, almost all states with redfish have designated conservative limits (ranging from one fish per day in Florida to five in Georgia) and slot size limits designed to protect mature breeding fish. The problem is too many anglers. Redfish are a popular, readily accessible quarry that attracts hundreds of thousand of fishermen every season.

In contrast to issues like inshore habitat degradation by agricultural runoff, the solution to this problem is obvious and fairly painless. I am old enough to remember when anglers routinely kept legal limits of everything they caught, and the dismay that greeted the first catch-and-release regulations in freshwater. However, catch-and-release practices quickly became standard on most trout streams, cheered on by no one as enthusiastically as the anglers they restricted. Catch-and-release has been much slower to evolve in marine waters for various reasons, including tradition and the superior table quality of many saltwater game fish. Nonetheless, the same year sport anglers killed and ate a half-million redfish, they also released five times that many. That's a good start. Catch-and release restrictions should be predicated on biology rather than political correctness. Whenever the sport harvest becomes numerically significant to fish stocks, they offer an attractive management option.

The point of this digression is to emphasize that no individual or organization can claim a flawless record on behalf of wildlife and the environment—not me, not Ducks Unlimited, not the Sierra Club. The key is to be candid about our historical shortcomings and creative about our solutions, even when they hurt a little. Wildlife deserves nothing less.

Back on the Columbia, Lori, hunting partner Michael Crowder, and I continued to watch birds come and go. I'd killed some bluebills and a redhead by that time but still had some room in my limit. Some of the shots looked tempting, but I was waiting for a special bird.

"Drake can!" Michael whispered suddenly from the stern.

"I think it's a redhead," I replied; the bird was still well off in the distance.

"No it's not!" Michael insisted. "It's . . . "

By then the bird had turned broadside in its first circuit about the decoys, and I could tell that Michael was right. I let the single circle us twice before I rose, drove the shotgun's barrels farther out in front of the bird than I ever imagined possible, and slapped the trigger. Time stood still as the shot column spread out across the water, and then the drake collapsed.

"We've still got room for a few more birds," Michael pointed out as I unloaded my second barrel. "And remember: We get two cans this year."

I literally couldn't remember the last time I'd killed a canvasback. Even when it became legal to shoot one per day again, I'd held my fire on the rare occasions when I had an opportunity to shoot one. Aware of that year's robust flight numbers, I had no regrets about the lone drake bobbing on the chop. But would two canvasbacks really be better than one?

"I'm happy to stay if you want," I told Michael. "But I'm done for the day." And why not? I had what I'd come for: an affirmation of five decades worth of successful waterfowl conservation.

PART TWO

Sportsmen and Wildlife Today

STANDING UP FOR WILDLIFE

I t's a crisp winter evening in central Montana, in many ways an inauspicious time for hunting and angling enthusiasts. Cold weather shut the local fly fishing down months ago, and save for mountain lions, there won't be anything to hunt until turkey season opens in early April. Nonetheless, I'm feeling very much the sportsman as I shuck my wool coat and escort Lori through the door to join in what passes quite successfully as a major social event in our rural town of five thousand: the annual fund-raising banquet sponsored by our local chapter of Ducks Unlimited.

The ducks themselves have long since headed south, except for the hardy mallards that overwinter on the ice-resistant spring creeks nearby, but you'd be hard-pressed to prove that here in the dining room of the local Eagles Club tonight. Waterfowl art crowds the walls, inviting bids during the upcoming benefit auction. Some of the paintings are serialized prints by nationally renowned artists, while others are originals by local painters whose reputations barely extend to the borders of the state. To my eye the quality in both groups ranges from the trite to the inspiring, but the underlying cause is common to them all.

Even though events like this exhausted the wall space inside our own home years ago, I find myself lingering in front of a First of Nation duck stamp print from Italy, of all places. (Yes, Ding Darling's inspired notion from the 1930s has spread that far. If only more ideas from Washington had represented American ideals abroad so successfully.) Save for the faint outline of Renaissance architecture in the background, the exquisitely rendered pintail pair could be settling into my own decoy spread at first light.

A quick circuit about the room establishes the eclectic nature of the crowd. As longtime local residents, Lori and I know virtually everybody here, and we've soon exchanged greetings with everyone from bankers and cowboys to nurses and teachers, men and women, old and young. I've made a point to run down both our local game wardens, as well as biologists from the state Department of Fish, Wildlife & Parks and the local branch of the U.S. Fish and Wildlife Service. Lori and I fit into the mix in equally disjointed fashion: doctor and nurse to some; writer and photographer, neighbors, and hunting partners to others. Somehow, the small talk always turns quickly to ducks, hunting, and wildlife.

When I finally retreat to a quiet corner and survey the crowd, I quickly realize what a remarkable phenomenon is taking place all around me. This isn't Hollywood; no one has come to see and be seen, and no one really cares about the banquet meal brewing back in the kitchen. Everyone here tonight has come because they care about ducks—not just about shooting them (although almost everyone present is a duck hunter), but about the future of waterfowl and the places they call home.

In 1832 Colonel William Slater established the nation's first sportsmen's club. Located south of Baltimore, the Carroll's Island Club allowed wealthy urban hunters a chance to monopolize some exclusive waterfowl hunting and enjoy it in relative luxury. Activism on behalf of wildlife was simply not part of the club's agenda, and the sportsmen's clubs that followed remained similarly oblivious for several decades. When the number of clubs exploded later in the nineteenth century, they finally began to become involved in environmental affairs. The concern they expressed on behalf of America's vanishing wildlife was genuine and often quite articulate, but that concern was mostly directed toward local issues, and despite their best intentions, the clubs lacked political clout.

By the end of a decade's worth of inspired activism during the 1930s, all that had changed. Sportsmen had become organized on the national level, and the increasingly sophisticated political influence they wielded began to produce real benefits for wildlife. Beginning with Ducks Unlimited in 1937, these organizations grew into the loose coalition of sportsman-driven groups working effectively on behalf of wildlife today. While space precludes an examination of all such organizations, it would be impossible to understand the current status of wildlife in America without reviewing a representative sample.

Ducks Unlimited

A product of the activist 1930s, Ducks Unlimited (DU) and its leadership quickly established an agenda that became a model for dozens of similar groups to follow. From the time of George Bird Grinnell through the passage of the Lacey Act, sporting conservationists had devoted most of their collective effort to combating poaching, eliminating market hunting, and the enforcement of existing wildlife laws. As progressive legislation began to address those concerns effectively, the drought-induced waterfowl catastrophe of the early Great Depression years established a new paradigm: the paramount importance of healthy habitat to the future of wildlife (as, to give credit where it's due, Theodore Roosevelt had recognized a generation before). Spawned from the Dust Bowl debacle, DU made habitat its prime concern from the start.

Beginning with its Big Grass Marsh project in Manitoba, DU had protected 150,000 acres of wetlands by the end of its first year of operation. By 2007 DU had funded some 68,000 similar projects involving waterfowl habitat in Canada, the United States, and Mexico, conserving twelve million acres of wetlands in the process. The scope of action taken on those projects varied considerably. In some cases, DU leased or purchased critical habitat outright to save it from development unfriendly to wildlife. In other cases, DU simply provided money, education, and expertise to landowners so they could maintain habitat themselves.

The organization now has over 800,000 members throughout North America (the overwhelming majority of them hunters), including 45,000 volunteers responsible for fund-raising efforts like our local banquet (4,600 of which now take place annually). In 2007 DU raised $213 million; 87 percent of these revenues go directly to funding restoration and preservation of wildlife habitat.

A group this large and well-funded represents a significant measure of lobbying clout, and the DU leadership has used its influence to considerable political advantage. The organization provided key support for the legislation authorizing the Conservation Reserve Program (CRP), the Wetlands Reserve Program (WRP), and North American Wetlands Conservation Act (NAWCA), all important conservation measures that likely would not have seen the light of day without support from sportsmen's groups.

But even encouraging numbers become numbing after a while. It's equally important to address some of the more intangible aspects of DU's success. While sportsmen have always been an opinionated and contentious lot, the DU leadership has done an admirable job of avoiding the bickering and factional infighting that have compromised the mission of so many conservation organizations. They've accomplished this goal by avoiding needless confrontations (DU has never filed a lawsuit) and staying on message consistently: It's all about habitat. By refusing to engage other issues, the organization has remained open and accessible to all who share concern for the common cause.

Many hunters today feel uncomfortable with the "Big Tent Theory," as the impetus to uncritical consensus among sportsmen's ranks has become known, arguing that the simple purchase of a hunting license does not establish brotherhood, especially with those who would abuse the privilege. However, when the goal is as worthy and the message as consistent as DU's, committed unity of purpose makes overwhelming good sense.

Rocky Mountain Elk Foundation

Earlier chapters have already traced a sine wave in the well-being of North America's elk population, from widespread abundance at the time of European colonization, through critical decline and complete extirpation from much of its original range by the beginning of the twentieth century, to an encouraging rebound as modern principles of game management began to evolve. Despite that gratifying recovery, some knowledgeable sportsmen recognized that it wasn't nearly gratifying enough.

In 1984 an eclectic, blue-collar group of four elk-hunting enthusiasts met in Troy, Montana, to do something about it. A pastor, a real estate agent, a logger, and a drive-in owner, the foursome lacked just about everything needed to start a national conservation program, including organizational expertise, media savvy, and funding. Undaunted, they borrowed enough money to print and distribute forty-three thousand flyers outlining their plan to start an organization dedicated to securing more habitat for elk. Four years later, the Rocky Mountain Elk Foundation (RMEF) had a staff of twelve, thirty-two thousand members, seventy chapters, and a new home in Missoula.

In order to appreciate the RMEF's accomplishments, one must appreciate the needs of the elk. Some of North America's indigenous wild mammals are highly adaptable species that not only survived but thrived in proximity to human development. Others, like the bison, have specific habitat requirements that conflict directly with modern land use practices, while others still, like the grizzly, simply can't tolerate human presence. Elk fall somewhere in the middle. Agriculture can provide beneficial food sources for elk (to the frequent dismay of farmers and ranchers), but they still require large, undisturbed tracts of security cover, and since they are seasonally migratory, they need lots of room to live.

Over the last two decades, the RMEF has taken ambitious steps to provide it. The organization has experienced substantial growth—to some 155,000 members in 550 chapters—and the fund-raising and corporate sponsorship that accompanied that growth has allowed protection and enhancement of over 5.4 million acres of elk habitat, a number that will become increasingly significant in the face of expanded energy development in the West.

Currently, elk populations are at or near historic highs in most western states, but the interface between extractive industry and sensitive species like elk seldom turns out well for wildlife. Tracking studies confirm that elk will vacate areas in the face of development even if that means relocating to otherwise inferior habitat. Build enough roads in the backcountry, and elk will eventually run out of places to hide. Establishing adequate reservoirs and corridors of security cover, as the RMEF has done, helps eliminate that threat to their well-being.

RMEF funding and biological expertise played a crucial role in what may be an even more impressive accomplishment: restoration of North American elk to their original range. Hunters of my generation once regarded the elk as an exclusive inhabitant of the Mountain West, despite abundant evidence proving that assumption historically inaccurate. Working in conjunction with state wildlife agencies, the RMEF helped spearhead the successful reintroduction of elk to eastern locations that hadn't seen free-ranging wapiti for over a century. As a result of these efforts, healthy wild elk populations now inhabit a number of eastern and midwestern states.

Not every elk hunter always agrees with every position the RMEF has taken. Such differences are inevitable among groups as opinionated as sportsmen, which is why organizational leaders who can get sportsmen to agree long enough to accomplish anything deserve so much respect. Such disagreement shouldn't compromise regard for what the RMEF has done. When I was growing up, the idea of elk in Kentucky was unthinkable. But it's reality today, and everyone there who has thrilled to the sound of a bull elk bugling in the fall owes it to themselves and the elk to acknowledge those who made that experience possible, whether they hunt or not.

Trout Unlimited

Most of America's wild fisheries suffered through the same cycle of plenty, decimation, and gradual recovery as its populations of game birds and animals, and anglers played an equally significant role in that recovery. While hunters have attracted most of the misguided animosity the public and the media have directed toward sportmen's pursuits, anglers have started to receive their share from the radical fringe of the animal rights movement—witness the recent efforts by People for the Ethical Treatment of Animals (PETA) to rechristen fish "sea kittens."

The history of American anglers' attempts to salvage their declining fisheries began with yet another individual giant in the conservation field. Born in 1817, Seth Green preceded George Bird Grinnell by a generation. An avid angler, he recognized an impending disaster in the freshwater fisheries along the eastern seaboard and devoted a truly remarkable amount of time and energy to salvaging them through aquaculture, a science that he practically invented. Unfortunately, despite his personal dedication and energy, Green had it wrong from the start. The problem wasn't the lack of fish, but the deteriorating quality of fish habitat.

Green's paradigm—raise fish in hatcheries, release them into the water, and let anglers catch them—persisted for a hundred years, bogging state wildlife agencies down in efforts to rear artificial fish that diluted superior native genetics and distracted attention from the real problem of habitat degradation. Sportsmen of the times deserve their share of blame for allowing themselves to be bought off so cheaply by hatchery fish. Fortunately for the sake of this book's thesis, however, anglers also deserve due credit for helping reverse that sorry state of affairs.

In 1959 a small group of anglers gathered in Grayling, Michigan, to share their concerns over these issues, particularly their state's promotion of hatchery fish at the expense of native trout populations. That meeting provided the groundwork for the organization that would become Trout Unlimited (TU). The group emphasized the importance of scientifically sound resource management from the start. As Dr. Casey Westell, TU's first president, put it: "One of our more important objectives is to develop programs and recommendations based on the very best thinking available. In all matters of trout management, we want to know that we are substantially correct, both morally and biologically."

TU's mission statement reads: "To conserve, protect and restore North America's coldwater fisheries and their watersheds." (Reflecting the angling interests of its founders, the *coldwater* qualification politely establishes that the organization is more concerned with trout than catfish.) Their first policy success took place in the group's home state when, in 1963, they persuaded the Michigan Department of Natural Resources to stop stocking trout and direct their efforts to the habitat issues that really mattered.

At the time, sportsmen around the country were finally beginning to recognize the futility of hatchery programs. Inspired by events in Michigan, this new awareness, often far ahead of the attitudes held by their own entrenched state fisheries biologists, helped TU grow rapidly to its current level of some 150,000 volunteers in 400 chapters around the nation.

Both their record of accomplishment and their current agenda may be more diversified than that of any other organization profiled in this chapter. TU has successfully lobbied for the removal of outmoded dams blocking anadromous fish runs on the East Coast and secured habitat protection for numerous pristine drainages in the West. Often in partnership with other organizations, TU has been a consistent and potent lobbying force in Congress, helping to insure that wildlife provisions aren't gutted from complex legislation like the federal Farm Bill. TU has played a key role in organizing broad-based opposition to Alaska's proposed Pebble Mine, a potential ecological disaster that threatens Bristol Bay salmon runs, the most robust in the world. In this capacity, TU has shown a notable ability to unite not just recreational anglers, but interests as diverse as commercial fishermen and Alaska Natives justifiably concerned about the proposed project's impact upon their traditional way of life.

There has always been a certain amount of back and forth in the American angling community between trout enthusiasts (who, among other things, tend to fish with fly rods and release their catch) and anglers interested in warm-water species like bass and walleye (who generally fish with conventional tackle and fry fish for dinner). The ability of TU's leadership to bridge such gaps and form alliances across a broad spectrum of the outdoor community may be the group's defining organizational trait.

Such politics can make strange bedfellows. Growing up in the Pacific Northwest after my family moved there from upstate New York in 1963, I learned to regard commercial fishermen as enemies who intercepted "our" salmon and steelhead before they reached the streams we loved to fish. That same perception followed me north to Alaska, where I witnessed endless rounds of argument over the allocation of Kenai River king salmon between sport and commercial interests (among many examples). I credit TU with helping both parties to this longstanding dispute recognize that the real threat to wild runs of anadromous fish comes from environmental factors that threaten everyone's interests.

And as just one example of its response to the collapse of the salmon fishery in California and Oregon, TU organized an unlikely coalition of recreational and commercial anglers, fish dealers, and California vintners into its "Have Your Salmon and Eat It Too" campaign, designed to emphasize the value of wild salmon (and the biological, environmental, and culinary inferiority of their artificially farmed counterparts) throughout the entire economy of the West Coast.

Pheasants Forever

In 1982 a group of sportsmen concerned about declining pheasant populations met in Saint Paul, Minnesota, to address the issue. Inspired by the example Ducks Unlimited had set by spearheading the conservation of waterfowl and their habitat, they founded a new organization dedicated to supporting the same goals for upland birds: Pheasants Forever (PF).

When I was a kid in upstate New York, pheasant "conservation" consisted of state-sponsored releases of pen-raised birds prior to the upland bird season, one reason my father and I spent each fall hunting wild grouse and woodcock instead. Even as an eager kid, I recognized that there was something just plain wrong with pen-raised pheasants. A leftover relic dating back to Seth Green's early attempts at aquaculture, this model—planting artificially raised game birds into inadequate habitat—was expensive, futile (pen-raised birds provide ecosystems little more than brief banquets for predators), and biologically deleterious (because of the artificial introduction of inferior avian genetics).

Eschewing the planted bird model, PF leadership recognized the primary importance of habitat from the start, and has successfully addressed habitat issues on numerous fronts. Partnering with private landowners, the organization's Habitat Forever teams provide technical expertise, manpower, equipment, and funding at no cost to farmers and ranchers interested in benefiting wildlife for a variety of reasons ranging from pure altruism to a desire to provide family and friends with better bird hunting. These teams currently operate in ten states, predominantly in the Midwest.

Utilizing combined funding from state wildlife departments and federal (USDA) sources, the organization also sponsors Farm Bill Biologists, professional sources of technical habitat management expertise who have worked on over five thousand local projects. PF programs have improved wildlife habitat on more than five million acres of farmland. Like DU, PF also funds the outright purchase of some critical habitat. Approximately one thousand such acquisitions now total over a hundred thousand acres. Finally, PF has lobbied heavily to ensure adequate consideration for wildlife in numerous important pieces of federal legislation, including federal farm bills that often disguise "sleeper" sources of important funding for wildlife. PF has been especially vigorous in its support for the Conservation Reserve Program.

Structurally, PF recognized the importance of grassroots organization in the heartland from the start. Nationally endorsed, locally driven fund-raisers have always been an important source of revenue for conservation groups, but PF has consistently kept locally raised money in its community of origin for the benefit of local habitat projects at the direction of local leadership. Over 27,000 such projects have been completed to date. Sensitivity to local needs and priorities has no doubt contributed to the organization's rapid growth. PF currently has 115,000 members distributed among 650 local chapters in all fifty states.

PF has always taken the position that sound habitat restoration benefits many forms of wildlife in addition to the nominal target species. PF isn't releasing pen-raised pheasants into the wild so people can shoot them; it is directing its efforts to the restoration of native prairie grassland habitat threatened by agriculture and development—a worthwhile conservation goal even if the ring-necked pheasant had never made it across the Pacific to Owen Denny's Oregon farm in 1872. A long list of indigenous wildlife species benefits from these restoration projects, including raptors and mammalian predators—and PF (like DU, but in contrast to some other sportsman-driven organizations) has never advocated the deliberate destruction of predators for the benefit of "more desirable" species.

Paradoxically, the politically driven, apparently green movement to develop sources of biofuels from the American heartland promises a whole new round of threats to grassland habitat. American sportsmen—and American wildlife—will need groups like PF more than ever in the coming battle.

Theodore Roosevelt Conservation Partnership

With Ducks Unlimited serving as an effective prototype, the modern model of the sportsman-driven wildlife advocacy group—an organization focused on the habitat needs of a given species or group of related species—has admirably served wildlife constituents across a broad spectrum ranging from Atlantic salmon to North American wild sheep. As effective as that model has proven, other sportsmen have recognized the need to think outside that well-established box, especially in the political arena.

In 2002 a group of movers and shakers led by the late attorney Jim Range, an avid sportsman and Washington, D.C. veteran who served as chief council to Senate Majority Leader Howard Baker before entering the private sector, founded the Theodore

Roosevelt Conservation Partnership (TRCP) to create a unified political voice for sportsmen with varying backgrounds and concerns. The TRCP was born from a political failure. As Range recounted in our recent interview, conservation programs need stable funding to be effective. Much of Pittman-Robertson's success derives from its status as a formula program, which allows funding to bypass the politically charged appropriations process. During the Clinton administration, Range, among others, worked to secure the same status for monies derived from the Conservation Reinvestment Act (CRA), which directs a portion of the revenue from energy development on the outer continental shelf to conservation purposes. But politics as usual in congressional appropriations committees prevented that from happening.

An irate Range noted recent media and public relations success by groups like the Sierra Club and told his colleagues, "If we'd had that expertise, we would have won on CRA." He then set about organizing the TRCP to provide it. TRCP leadership recognized from the start that many of the most important battles would be won or lost in the halls of Congress rather than in the field, and that one unified, carefully reasoned voice could represent the interests of sportsmen—and wildlife—more effectively than many divided efforts. While that principle represented sound political judgment, the devil, as always, would be in the details. In its first years of life, the TRCP has shown a remarkable knack for getting them right.

The TRCP brought its own style to the table from the beginning. Instead of initiating an aggressive media campaign for membership and funds, the organization recognized that much of that work had already been done. Accordingly, they enlisted a group of like-minded nonprofits such as Trout Unlimited and Pheasants Forever, supplemented by a roster of corporate partners. In a demonstration of political savvy, they noted that 70 percent of labor union members hunt or fish, and promptly established their Union Sportsman Alliance, which now has thousands of members. Leadership also deliberately avoided taking polarizing positions on any issue. While that decision might have come at the cost of some credibility among more strident wildlife advocates, it also made good political sense.

So did its fundamental approach to accomplishing its goals, which were political right from the start. Rather than fragmenting its efforts pursuing more glamorous and controversial issues, TRCP leadership chose to address one or two major (if sometimes boring) pieces of legislation at a time and work behind the scenes in Washington to turn the final product into law favorable to wildlife. They started with the 2004 Federal Highway Bill, an uninspiring venue for legislative action that many conservation groups all but ignored. But by that time the TRCP was representing nine million sportsmen around the country, a number that deserved congressional attention—and got it. The bill eventually passed with $2 billion earmarked for wildlife.

The TRCP has regularly repeated that pattern of quiet, behind-the-scenes success. They have lobbied hard—and largely if not always successfully—for continued funding for the Conservation Reserve Program (CRP), and recently fought (along with TU, DU, PF, and other sportsman-led groups) to eliminate a worrisome provision in the 2008 Farm Bill that would have allowed contracted farmers to terminate their agreements prematurely and convert CRP land to lucrative new alternatives like biofuel development at the cost of millions of acres of wildlife habitat.

The TRCP is currently focusing on just a handful of other issues, including fossil fuel development, mining law reform, and the designation of roadless areas. None of these causes is as sexy as saving whales or wolves, but all carry tremendous implications for wildlife. Done right, this legislation could secure critical habitat for generations to come. Done wrong—as many powerful interests would just love to see happen—it could mean disaster, not just for one species or one watershed, but for all American wildlife.

In addition to its legislative savvy, the TRCP has demonstrated fresh organizational instincts. Recognizing that conservation groups—including all of the worthwhile organizations profiled here—are fundamentally competing with each other for members and dollars, the TRCP rose above the fray and let its nonprofit partners worry about members and dues. There's no such thing as a paid membership in the TRCP, although anyone can become an individual partner with the click of a computer mouse.

Politics has always involved the art of compromise, and willingness to do so will inevitably alienate some members of the conservation community. When does expediency justify compromise of theoretical principle? Can an organization that includes powerful corporate sponsors be trusted to confront industry when necessary? Only time will tell. In the meantime, the TRCP is sponsoring smart people to digest thousands of pages of arcane legislation, parsing them for opportunities to benefit wildlife—and the potential disasters that others love to bury deep in complex legislation where they hope no one will notice them.

Backcountry Hunters and Anglers

Just as sportsmen organize around concern for a given species or geographic area, they also group according to their personal interests in the outdoors, often to the detriment of their ability to operate with consistent political effect. Hunters and anglers don't always mix well, for example, except in the case of individuals devoted to both forms of outdoor sport. Within the hunting community, big game hunters don't always share common interests with those who hunt waterfowl and upland birds. Among those who hunt big game, distinctions arise between bow hunters and rifle hunters, who often wind up competing with each other for preferential treatment in the structure of hunting seasons. Among bow hunters, strong differences have evolved between those who hunt with modern, technically advanced archery equipment and those who eschew technology in favor of traditional, unadorned longbows and recurves. And so on and so on and so on . . .

That's not all bad by any means, but there also must be room at the table for outdoorsmen of various inclinations who share certain core values no matter what they carry with them when they head to the field. Another relatively new arrival on the scene,

Backcountry Hunters and Anglers (BHA), was founded in 2004 with just that goal in mind. Membership is open without distinction to hunters and anglers with many specific sporting interests who share a common goal: the preservation of pristine wildlife habitat and its defense against such contemporary threats as irresponsible energy development and abuse of the backcountry by the unauthorized intrusion of off-road vehicles (ORVs).

The introduction to recent BHA testimony before the U.S. Senate Committee on Energy and Natural Resources provides a concise summary of the organization's mission: "Backcountry Hunters and Anglers is a national organization of outdoor enthusiasts who take pride in the tradition, challenge and solitude of America's backcountry. Founded around an Oregon campfire, we now have members in 43 states. BHA is a 501(c) (3) non-profit organization that works to conserve big, natural habitat and healthy rivers and streams. We work so our kids and grandkids are free to enjoy the high-quality hunting and fishing we cherish."

Young and still growing rapidly, BHA has employed its own version of the partnership model advocated by the Theodore Roosevelt Conservation Partnership to increase its political impact on a number of western regional issues, often in conjunction with Trout Unlimited. This kind of teamwork led to the successful preservation of the 13,700-acre Copper-Salmon Wilderness Area in Oregon. BHA is also part of a TU-led coalition fighting to safeguard wildlife interests in a million acres of Wyoming backcountry facing accelerated energy development. The Alaska BHA chapter has taken on the Pebble Mine project and risked the wrath of many Alaskan hunters by criticizing that state's recent attempts to increase moose and caribou numbers through the deliberate destruction of predators like bears and wolves.

While these habitat and wilderness campaigns enjoy broad-based support from many groups, BHA has virtually adopted as its own one orphan issue of particular growing concern to western sportsmen and other wildlife enthusiasts: ORV abuse. Admittedly, and to our collective shame, sportsmen across the nation have hardly taken a unified position on the matter. Hunting from

ORVs is a way of life in some parts of the country, and industry-sponsored outdoor television shows continue to tout their utility while dismissing their epidemic abuse as the work of the usual suspects for most environmental misdeeds: "a few bad apples."

But westerners know better, simply because they have more pristine backcountry at risk. Even when wilderness area designations and Forest Service travel plans prohibit ORV use, enforcement is a low priority that too often falls between the cracks of various jurisdictional agencies. Meanwhile, illegal ORV use continues to destroy habitat and displace wildlife, creating proven adverse effects upon species like elk and causing dismay not just among hunters and anglers, but hikers and other backcountry recreationists as well.

The issue may seem obscure to outdoorsmen from parts of the country that lack large tracts of unspoiled land, but ORV abuse is serious business to ethical western sportsmen, as Oregon backcountry hunter and current BHA president Mike Beagle recently explained to me: "All of our members tell a familiar story—working hard and playing by the rules—only to have illegal or inappropriate riders on ORVs shatter their experience, ruin their stalks, frighten their pack strings, and damage habitat. I've experienced these violations firsthand on the Green Tops, BLM land that I've visited and hunted in southwest Oregon since I was eleven. It's pretty pathetic to know that a climb that took me forty-five minutes on foot as a kid is too much to ask of some adults now."

While a number of sportsmen's groups have expressed varying degrees of concern about ORV abuse, that concern has all too often been tepidly couched in industry-approved terms implying that the problems reside with an irresponsible few (never mind that *all* the activities referenced above are illegal). Meanwhile, many environmentally focused wildlife advocacy groups feel they have more pressing issues to face as they battle to preserve entire watersheds and mountain ranges from development. BHA has chosen to confront the issue head-on.

In addition to support for the usual bills and testimony before the usual committees, BHA has a uniquely powerful tool at its disposal: peer pressure. In the West, where outsiders, government agencies, and environmental activists are all greeted with a certain universal suspicion, it is one thing for an illegal ORV rider to face sanction from one of those parties and quite another to confront the righteous anger of another local hunter or angler. Enough of that and the illegal backcountry ORV may go the way of the punt gun and live decoys.

American Prairie Foundation

And now another departure from the formula: a new organization of tremendous potential benefit to sportsmen and wildlife that didn't begin life as a sportsman's group at all—and still isn't, at least in the conventional sense.

The idea of creating a prairie grassland reserve to reproduce the unique North American savannah habitat Lewis and Clark found when they crossed the plains floated around eastern Montana for decades, to the general derision of the ranchers inhabiting the area. By 1996 The Nature Conservancy had pinpointed a sparsely settled section of eastern Montana north of the Missouri River as the optimal location for the concept, but the project never got off the ground. In 2000 a team from the World Wildlife Federation reopened the discussion and decided that a freestanding, independent, nonprofit organization offered the best chance of bringing the ambitious project to fruition. The American Prairie Foundation (APF) was formed, and Montana native Sean Gerrity became the new group's first board member.

Initially, the local reception was cool. Many area ranchers viewed the group as a threat to their traditional way of life, and they weren't the only skeptics. The idea of wealthy out-of-state interests buying up large tracts of remote Montana ranch land didn't sit well with most local sportsmen, who had seen plenty of that already as western land-use practices changed over the preceding decade.

Fortunately, the APF leadership recognized the importance of local cooperation to its goals. When I sat down with Gerrity, by then the APF executive director, he explained that the organization's mission was to restore a large segment of Northern Plains prairie habitat to its original state on a contiguous tract of land large enough to comprise its own legitimate ecosystem. This ambitious plan would allow the re-creation of wildlife populations equivalent to what Lewis and Clark encountered, including herds of free-ranging, genetically pure bison. As a resident of the area and student of its ecology and wildlife, I certainly admired that goal.

But I'd also seen my share of outside interests arrive in Montana with their own agendas and little regard for local sensibilities. While I've visited more of the world than most eastern Montana ranchers, I still share some of the prevailing local xenophobia when it comes to outside money, land use, and wildlife. When I began to express those concerns, my conversation with Gerrity grew even more interesting.

He began by articulating an undeniable demographic fact. The area the APF had targeted for restoration is one of the most geographically isolated, sparsely populated areas in the continental United States. Since the early days of the homestead era more than a century before, its economy, such as it is, has depended on family cattle ranches, which are becoming economically nonviable there for a variety of reasons. The area had been losing population at the rate of 10 percent annually for decades. As more ranches failed, someone was going to buy these properties and convert them to other uses. The questions became *who* and *what,* and the more we talked, the more pessimistic I became about the default possibilities.

The APF had anticipated local objections to their mission. The area had already experienced substantial conflict between local ranchers and government following the Clinton administration's designation of a nearby segment of the Missouri Breaks as a national monument. The possibility of losing property tax revenues, critical to the support of struggling rural schools, had been one of their more concrete concerns. Gerrity explained that as a nonprofit organization, the APF was not required to pay property taxes, but they were voluntarily doing so anyway.

What about the Montana ranch community's deep-seated concern about brucellosis and buffalo? All buffalo introduced to APF property were tested and retested, with results made available to the public. What about wolves and grizzlies, both as popular among Montana ranchers as brucellosis? Maybe someday . . . but not until the time was right.

And what about hunting? If the goal was the restoration of Lewis and Clark–era prairie habitat, that habitat included human predators. Gerrity smiled. A Montana native himself, hunting is as much a part of his life as it is of mine. APF projections call for appropriately regulated public hunting in all parts of the reserve where such activities do not conflict with biological goals.

I now serve on the APF Advisory Council and the committee designed to integrate appropriate public hunting into the APF mission. The organization has never wavered from that commitment— or from its willingness to respect other local values. Over the course of many meetings, I have spoken with APF members and supporters who are sportsmen, an even greater number who do not hunt but are interested in learning about it and supportive of its place in the APF, and a few who clearly oppose hunting. So far, these diverging views have not compromised the organization's commitment to wildlife, or to those who enjoy wild places in a variety of ways.

The APF goal remains an intact prairie ecosystem of some five million acres, which would make it the country's largest wildlife reserve. This will be accomplished through the purchase of private property from willing sellers and partnership with state and local agencies (the proposed reserve borders the huge Charles M. Russell Wildlife Refuge and includes vast tracts of BLM land now devoted to cattle grazing). The first bison transplants have already taken place, and the animals are successfully reproducing.

While the inclusion of the APF—an organization not primarily driven by sportsmen—may seem an anomaly in this discussion, it represents an important example of the kind of partnership the conservation community badly needs today. Sportsmen are fond of accusing non-hunters of bias, but we need to recognize that we're guilty of it ourselves and make more direct attempts to work with conservation organizations that aren't directly driven by sportsmen. Non-hunting conservationists willing to partner with sportsmen will accomplish more than those who do not. And if the diverse segments of the APF leadership had assumed a siege mentality and retreated to their respective corners from the start, the organization never would have risen from the ground. Phillips County ranches would still be failing, wildlife would still be competing with domestic livestock on public property, and what private land did sell would have become part of the ongoing commercialization of the West's wildlife. Surely we can do better.

It is interesting to compare this record of accomplishment on behalf of wildlife to that of other non-sporting organizations ostensibly espousing the same goals, particularly those that actively campaign against hunting. Ducks Unlimited plows 87 percent of its annual fund-raising directly back into wildlife habitat and conservation, Pheasants Forever 91 percent, the Rocky Mountain Elk Foundation nearly 95 percent. How do those figures contrast with the efforts of anti-hunting organizations that claim to represent the best interests of wildlife?

The Humane Society of the United States (HSUS) campaigns to "save" the West's feral horses—an introduced, alien species causing severe environmental degradation that threatens critical habitat for native animals like desert bighorn sheep and mule deer—while a review of that organization's literature reveals *no* investment in wildlife habitat.

Greenpeace continues to conduct a controversial, well-publicized effort to "save" whales from the Japanese whaling fleet in the South Pacific using confrontational tactics that violate maritime law. No matter what one's views on commercial whaling, global warming and the pollution of the seas obviously pose a greater threat than Japanese whalers to the long-term survival of cetaceans. Wouldn't it make more sense to turn off the television cameras and redirect those efforts toward the real environmental threat to these species?

The Fund for Animals (now partnered with the HSUS), a frequent plaintiff in frivolous anti-hunting lawsuits, touts causes like the "rescue" of various animals at its Black Beauty Ranch. Yet a search of its Web site reveals no habitat work for wildlife at all.

People for the Ethical Treatment of Animals (PETA) opposes angling just as virulently as it opposes hunting and actively campaigns against eating fish of any kind. Its efforts to preserve wild stocks of fish and the waters they inhabit? Nil.

Conflict between true conservationists and groups like these arises from a fundamental difference in philosophy. Animal rights advocates care about the status of individual animals. Conservationists care about populations of animals and the wild habitat necessary to sustain them. One can only appeal to the majority non-hunting public to discern who has made it possible for populations of wildlife to survive so that there are any individual wild animals left to care about. All parties to the debate are entitled to their opinions, including the most extreme anti-hunting animal rights organizations. But when it comes to public policy, the record clearly shows who has actually stood up for wildlife in the past, and who continues to do so today.

The list of modern sportsman-driven wildlife and habitat organizations is so long now that it's hard to believe it started with Ducks Unlimited barely one generation ago. These groups now champion the cause of species ranging from redfish to ruffed grouse. Some are still largely social, providing members an opportunity to interact with sportsmen of like mind while doing some worthwhile habitat work. Others have grown into formidable political forces, and wildlife needs that clout now more than ever.

We may have sent the market hunters packing years ago, but wildlife will always need a place to live. The dynamic tension between wildlife and development hasn't changed much since the Yellowstone Park Improvement Company tried to convert pristine wilderness into cash in 1882. Our society's default position will always be the policy that makes the most money for the best-connected interests, and lack of an effective counterforce would leave wildlife in a precarious position indeed.

This compendium of worthwhile organizations has grown into such an embarrassment of riches that it has become impossible for any individual sportsman to support them all. Most have to make hard choices based on species, geography, and organizational philosophy. We experience no small measure of guilt when the checking account is empty and worthwhile causes haven't received the membership renewals they deserve.

Of course, none of these well-intended organizations is beyond reproach. Aldo Leopold and Ducks Unlimited, of all parties, entered into a major policy dispute after the Second World War. Many hunters recently criticized the Boone and Crockett Club for certifying as a world record a Utah elk taken by a wealthy hunter who had purchased the state's Governor's Tag for six figures, allowing him to kill the animal with a modern rifle in an area that was otherwise restricted to hunters carrying bows and muzzle loaders. Others have expressed discomfort with the Rocky Mountain Elk Foundation's decision to allow ORV advertising in its magazine. Not even their strongest supporters can claim infallibility for any of these groups, but they can point to a solid record of activism on behalf of wildlife that's impossible to deny.

Enlightened self-interest drives these organizations at least as much as environmental idealism. Of course, Pheasants Forever supporters are willing to fund habitat improvement so the habitat will carry more pheasants that sportsmen can hunt in the fall. Once again—so what? A Ducks Unlimited project on the Canadian prairie accomplishes far more than the production of ducks. Healthy habitat does not discriminate among its occupants, which in this example would no doubt include a cast of characters ranging from shorebirds to muskrats. These species in turn can provide unlimited enjoyment for all manner of "non-consumptive wildlife users" (a bit of jargon employed here only with the greatest sense of irony). They deserve to know who made it possible.

MODERN WILDLIFE LEGISLATION

The first century of the American conservation movement depended heavily upon two sources for its hard-won successes: the personal vision of a few inspired pioneers and the passage of landmark pieces of legislation so well conceived and crafted that they withstood their inevitable challenges and became part of the foundation of our wildlife law. The generation of Americans born after the Second World War has yet to produce a Roosevelt, Leopold, or Grinnell, perhaps because we've entered an age in which organizations serve wildlife policy better than individuals. But my lifetime certainly has seen the passage of important wildlife legislation.

Will these statutes prove as important in the long run as the Lacey Act, the Migratory Waterfowl Treaty, and Pittman-Robertson? Only time will tell. But these laws are certainly helping wildlife today, and like their important predecessors, most came to pass largely as the result of organized sportsmen's efforts.

The Conservation Reserve Program

First authorized by Congress in 1985, the Conservation Reserve Program (CRP) has drawn wide praise as one of the most successful government programs to reach the American heartland in a generation. The interface between agriculture and wildlife is complex, and unfortunately farmers and wildlife advocates don't always find themselves on the same side of many issues. The CRP is nearly unique in the universal high praise it has earned from both parties. Nowadays its results have become so widely visible across the Midwest that its acronym has become a familiar part of the regional vocabulary, as in, "Go down the road two miles past that first section of CRP . . ."

A combination of factors led to the program's creation in 1985. A new cycle of drought had impacted wildlife and habitat: The spring U.S. Fish and Wildlife Service (USFWS) waterfowl survey that year indicated that populations of mallard, pintail, and teal were at thirty-year lows. Midwestern farmlands suffered from erosion. Commodity surpluses impacted agricultural prices, triggering expensive price-support subsidies. Introduced as part of the federal Farm Bill, the CRP program addressed all of these issues at once by paying farmers to take marginal cropland out of production and reseed it with various forms of native grasses, with the USDA helping to pay for the conversion.

The dense ground cover that replaced grain crops slowed erosion dramatically. Waterfowl and upland game birds (not to mention a host of other wildlife species ranging from songbirds to deer) received high-quality security cover and just the kind of edge habitat Aldo Leopold had touted fifty years earlier. Farmers received a stable source of income through ten- and fifteen-year CRP contracts, and the duration of those leases provided stability for the wildlife benefiting from the cover. Taxpayers got cleaner air, cleaner water, and healthier wildlife populations for the dollars they otherwise would have spent in commodity price supports. It may be theoretically impossible for any government program to produce nothing but winners, but the CRP comes as close as anything in my lifetime.

Simple numbers confirm the program's popularity among agricultural producers. By 2004 portions of nearly four hundred-thousand farms were enrolled in the CRP. Demand among farmers exceeded supply despite a generous national cap of over thirty-six million acres (established by Congress). The average ratio of applications to acceptances was three to one nationally, and much higher in Montana and the Dakotas.

Hard facts also confirmed the program's benefit to wildlife. One study conducted from 1992 to 1997 calculated a 46 percent increase in nesting success among five species of puddle ducks in terrain converted to CRP, and estimated a fall flight increase of over twelve million birds as a result. An Iowa study showed a 40 percent increase in successful brood production among pheasants nesting in large tracts of CRP as opposed to their usual limited fencerow habitat. Pheasant populations increased by more than 50 percent in large tracts of CRP. Non-game wildlife benefited as well: A 1995 North Dakota study predicted a population decline of nearly 20 percent among five species of indigenous prairie songbirds if CRP ground cover was lost.

Ongoing funding for the program requires regular reauthorization by Congress. While some details of the program—terms of the leases, the number of acres capped nationally—have changed since inception through this process, the CRP's basic provisions remain intact. However, congressional funding bills always represent an opportunity for competing political interests to vie for the same federal dollars, and no combination of logic, popularity, or proven results can ensure that any program emerges from the process unscathed. While individual farmers and the organizations that represent them have consistently supported the program, Big Agriculture—a powerful Capitol Hill lobby—sees it differently: Every acre of CRP is an acre taken out of crop production, impacting sales of everything from tractors to fertilizer.

It's virtually certain that the CRP wouldn't be providing over thirty-five million acres of prime wildlife habitat today without determined lobbying on its behalf by sportsmen and their representative organizations. A number of sportsman-driven groups have served as effective advocates for the CRP, none more vigorously or consistently than Ducks Unlimited, Pheasants Forever, and, more recently, the Theodore Roosevelt Conservation Partnership (all of whom have joined with some twenty other conservation organizations to form the Agriculture and Wildlife Working Group).

The sophisticated political maneuvering these groups have demonstrated in support of the CRP neatly demonstrates how much more effective modern sportsmen's groups have become as wildlife advocates since the days when George Grinnell and the Boone and Crockett Club were struggling to save Yellowstone and its bison. Even so, nice guys (and wildlife) often finish last in the hardball world of Washington politics. Bart James, Director of Agriculture Conservation policy for DU, recently spoke with me about the 2008 Farm Bill. "We didn't do as well as we wanted for wildlife," he wistfully acknowledged. "The CRP acreage cap was reduced from 39.2 to 32 million acres." One can only wonder what it might have been if sportsmen weren't standing up to the Big Agriculture lobby.

No program is perfect, including the CRP. One of its provisions allows farmers to hay or graze CRP grasslands during "emergencies," which usually means drought. Unfortunately, that's just when wildlife needs the security CRP cover provides the most. If a deal is a deal, this loophole is unsettling. It has even led to rare disputes among wildlife advocacy groups. James explained that since DU's mandate is to protect waterfowl, his group was willing—for the continued success of the overall program—to accept a compromise that prohibited emergency cutting before the end of the waterfowl nesting season, when ducks had already received maximum benefit from CRP ground cover. Pheasants Forever opposed that compromise out of commitment to its own mission, which includes providing upland birds adequate cover year-round. Even so, such differences of opinion represent relatively minor conflict in support of a program whose overall impact on wildlife and habitat has been overwhelmingly positive.

After more than two decades of success, the CRP now faces a challenge from an unexpected quarter: America's admirable impulse to develop biofuels as a clean alternative to foreign oil. Never mind that the numbers don't stand up to rigorous analysis—political business as usual threatens to drive the price of midwestern corn so high that the CRP will no longer be able to compete for what was formerly marginal cropland. While no one can predict how this conflict will play out, wildlife will certainly have to rely more than ever on organized sportsmen's groups to salvage one of the most successful programs our federal government has ever produced on its behalf.

North American Wetlands Conservation Act

First authorized by Congress in 1989, the North American Wetlands Conservation Act (NAWCA) was designed to provide funding to implement the North American Waterfowl Management Plan (NAWMP). Sportsmen's groups were instrumental in lobbying for the act's initial passage and subsequent reauthorizations. Federal funds for these purposes derive from a variety of sources including direct appropriations from Congress, penalties and fines collected for violations of the 1918 Migratory Bird Treaty Act (MBTA), excise taxes on small engines mandated by the 1950 Federal Aid in Sport Fish Restoration Act, and interest from the Pittman-Robertson Trust Fund. The NAWCA makes these funds available as matching grants to partnerships carrying out wetlands restoration projects in the United States, Canada, and Mexico that further the goals outlined by the NAWMP.

Congress has reauthorized the NAWCA several times, increasing its annual funding to its current level (authorized through 2012) of $75 million annually. The act requires that federal funds be matched at a ratio of at least one to one by project sponsors, which include state wildlife agencies, private industry, individuals, and sportsmen's groups like Ducks Unlimited. To date, the NAWCA has funded over 1,600 projects in all fifty states, Canada, and Mexico.

Wetlands Reserve Program

Despite the success of early wetlands conservation programs beginning in the 1930s, by midcentury the United States has lost nearly 50 percent of its original wetland habitat. First authorized by Congress in 1990, the Wetlands Reserve Program (WRP) represents a concerted national effort to restore wetlands previously converted to marginal agricultural use—precisely the same habitat problem identified by Ding Darling and his colleagues during the collapse of the continent's waterfowl population sixty years earlier.

Like the CRP, landowner participation is entirely voluntary, so its terms have to be friendly to agricultural interests. With a national cap of some 2.2 million acres, its scope is but a fraction of the CRP's in terms of total acreage. Nonetheless, because of the inherent importance of wetland habitat, its net benefit to wildlife is greater than those numbers suggest.

The mechanics of the program mirror the CRP's in many ways. Landowners who meet certain eligibility requirements apply to participate through the USDA. Applications are ranked and approved at the state level. Eligible lands must meet one of several criteria, and in general consist of former wetlands that have been drained for agricultural purposes but which could become suitable wildlife habitat with adequate restoration. When an application is approved, the landowner files a conservation easement (either thirty-year or permanent) at the local land records office. The USDA pays for up to 100 percent of the restoration costs. The landowner maintains title to the land and full control of all access.

Should public funds be used to foster what in many cases may turn into private wildlife projects? In the case of wetlands restored and protected through the WRP (and privately by DU projects, for that matter), biology largely renders the question moot. While wetland restoration positively affects multiple wildlife species, the major beneficiaries are migratory birds that will eventually move up or down the line without regard to private property boundaries, keeping them solidly in the public domain.

As with the CRP, the WRP accomplishes far more than providing more game birds for hunters every fall. Many "area-sensitive" species (those requiring large, contiguous tracts of suitable habitat) of non-game birds have benefited from WRP projects, including Swainson's warblers and swallow-tailed kites. The WRP has also contributed to the ongoing recovery of the Louisiana black bear, an isolated population listed as "threatened" by the USFWS.

During the first fifteen years of its life, the WRP rivaled the CRP in popularity among landowners, with applications exceeding available funds by a margin of three to one. That began to change in 2006, largely due to a new method of assessing the value of conservation easements as mandated by the Natural Resources Conservation Service, which administers the program. The moral of that story is simply that the work of the conservation lobby is never done.

It is no coincidence that two of the most significant pieces of recent wildlife legislation have specifically targeted wetlands restoration. Wetlands are uniquely critical to the well-being of American wildlife from a habitat standpoint, especially in the continent's interior. But politics is politics, and left to their own devices, politicians can be remarkably oblivious to the fine points of habitat management. The NAWCA and WRP stand as testimonials to the ever-increasing lobbying expertise of sportsmen's groups, particularly Ducks Unlimited.

Endangered Species Act

This statute is something of an anomaly in this discussion, and not just because of its presentation out of chronological order. In contrast to the programs just discussed, sportsmen did not play a crucial role in the passage of this sweeping measure. However, even a brief review of modern wildlife law can't ignore what may be the most far-reaching piece of wildlife legislation our government has ever enacted: the 1973 Endangered Species Act (ESA).

One hopes that no responsible citizen would quarrel with the basic principle underlying the ESA: that societies have a moral obligation to prevent whenever possible the permanent eradication of a species and its unique DNA, especially when threatened extinctions result from human activities. Indeed, if the ESA had been passed in 1800 instead of 1973, we would likely still be enjoying the company of the heath hen, Labrador duck, and passenger pigeon (not to mention the Carolina parakeet, the great auk, the plains grizzly . . .). Operating at its best, the ESA has likely prevented some such biological catastrophes already. And as a product of the Nixon administration, the simple fact of the ESA's passage raises the hope that the spirit of Theodore Roosevelt lurks somewhere in the heart of all politicians.

Nonetheless, few pieces of wildlife legislation have proved more controversial or aroused animosity from so many segments of American society. It's not hard to understand why. Programs like the CRP produce far more winners than losers. In contrast, saving endangered species—*all* endangered species, including dozens unfamiliar even to Americans knowledgeable about wildlife— often proves inconvenient, aggravating, and costly. The ESA has consistently drawn criticism from development forces and private-property rights advocates. Provisions that provide open invitations to lawsuits have complicated professional wildlife management and dramatically increased its cost as borne by the states. And in a classic illustration of the law of unintended consequences, ESA provisions have occasionally motivated some parties to *eliminate* habitat critical to threatened or endangered species in order to avoid running afoul of the law.

The ESA has certainly proved beneficial to the legal profession. Civil suits are inherently polarizing, and suits filed by environmental activist groups under ESA provisions, which often appear frivolous even when they aren't, explain much of the animosity toward the bill among the general public, with wildlife too often caught in the crossfire. Whatever their eventual benefit to conservation, such suits are expensive and time consuming to litigate. Much of that cost is borne by state and federal wildlife agencies, using limited dollars that could clearly do more good in other ways.

For all of these reasons, most sportsman-driven wildlife groups have eschewed filing civil suits, whether related to the ESA or otherwise. As Bart James of DU explains, "We prefer to work with incentives rather than lawsuits. Despite our size, DU only has two attorneys on staff. The organization has never filed a lawsuit against anyone." While some environmental activists might label that policy timid at best and a betrayal of principle at worst, it's also sound politics—and equally sound public relations.

All of which proves two things: There is no such thing as perfect legislation, and saving endangered species is a challenging task. A complete review of the ESA lies beyond the scope of this discussion. However, one element of this complex law sheds interesting light on the subject of sportsmen and their role in conservation.

The ESA is a lot like *War and Peace* and the Geneva Convention: Despite the number of people who talk about it, remarkably few have actually read it in its entirety. Concerned sportsmen should at least be interested in the roster of species listed as endangered or threatened. (This information is readily available through the USFWS Web site.) The list makes a number of points of general biological interest. The many names of obscure, endangered Hawaiian birds offers a testimonial to the consequences of thoughtlessly introducing predatory alien species to isolated island ecosystems, while the remarkable number of unfamiliar endangered bats, kangaroo rats, and darters shows how little many of us really know about the biosphere we call home.

Then there are the game species, collectively most striking by their absence. The American alligator and the grizzly in the Lower 48 have been listed and subsequently delisted (with currently ongoing litigation involving the latter), creating remarkable biological success stories of their own. Otherwise among big game animals, the only listings are for geographically isolated populations and subspecies: the Florida panther and Key deer, remnant populations of black bears in the Deep South, isolated bands of desert bighorn sheep in the West. No big game animal is listed as threatened or endangered across its range.

Among avian species that were ever regarded as game birds, only two varieties of eider (the spectacled and Steller's) and the Attwater prairie chicken are listed, and most American sportsmen have never hunted any of the three. Except for several species of sturgeon, all the game fish listed are salmonids, and the majority of them are anadromous populations in specific, limited drainages threatened by development.

These observations raise an interesting question. If sportsmen— and hunters in particular—are decimating North American wildlife populations as their critics claim, why don't the species they hunt or fish for appear on the comprehensive federal Endangered Species List?

OTHER LANDS, OTHER MODELS

P revious chapters concentrated on *American* sportsmen and wildlife, for several reasons. This is the venue of greatest interest to most of us, and nowhere else has the history of wildlife activism by sportsmen been more apparent or better documented. The core principles that evolved among American sportsmen and their nearby counterparts in Canada have produced the most effective and egalitarian system of wildlife management in the world. But wildlife is an international resource, and this book's title claims that sportsmen saved the world, not just their own backyards. The best way to appreciate the significance of wildlife management and conservation in North America may be to study how wildlife has fared in alternative settings.

The examples that follow largely reflect my own firsthand experience on the ground on other continents, where I found much to admire about some aspects of sportsmen's involvement in wildlife management. I also encountered ample cause for despair, which if nothing else provides a heightened appreciation of what sportsmen accomplished here during the last century and offers cautionary direction for North American sportsmen in the century to come.

Africa

With the exception of the commercially exploited elephant, wildlife populations in Africa's remote interior generally remained strong into the twentieth century, as Theodore Roosevelt documented during his post-presidency safari. The abundance of African wildlife at that late date reflects neither altruism nor sound wildlife management—malaria and trypanosomiasis simply kept European colonists and the modern firearms they carried from settling those areas extensively.

However, other parts of Africa, especially the Indian Ocean coast from what is now South Africa's Eastern Cape north to Mozambique, offered climate and terrain better suited to European interests, and colonists arrived there from England, Holland, and Portugal contemporaneously with European settlement of our own eastern seaboard. There, the time line of colonists' eventual impact on wildlife bears a striking resemblance to what was happening in North America at the same time.

No species demonstrates the impact of European arrival as dramatically as the African elephant. At the time of the first permanent settlement on the Cape by the Dutch East India Company in 1652, elephants were abundant in the region, but then European demand for elephant ivory, used for piano keys, billiard balls, and ornamentation, accelerated rapidly. The indigenous Khoi San, who did not traditionally hunt elephants, soon learned to trap them in pits and barter their ivory to the Dutch for trade goods. The Afrikaner *Voortrekkers* who radiated inland from the coast initially depended upon the ivory trade for their income while they were establishing farming communities.

To the north, Portuguese colonists exploited the elephant in similar fashion. During the nineteenth century, Mozambique's entire economy depended upon ivory. At the peak of the ivory trade from 1879 to 1883, Mozambique exported some 850,000 kilograms (two million pounds) of ivory to Europe annually.

As with the bison in North America, the resource could not endure such sustained commercial pressure. Elephants were gone from the Cape by the early 1800s. By 1875 they had been extirpated as far north as the Transvaal. That same year, a British observer in the interior of what is now Zimbabwe noted an abundance of elephants. Ten years later, he lamented that elephants could no longer be found at all in the same area.

Because their economic value invited early exploitation, elephants provide a dramatic example of wildlife's fall in Africa, but it was hardly the only one. Early Cape settlers found the dry veldt of South Africa's Karoo teeming with springbok, the swift, delicate gazelles that are now the country's national animals. Their exact numbers, like those of the American bison, remain difficult to determine, but they certainly numbered in the millions. As late as 1896 one observer described a herd fifteen miles wide and one hundred miles in length. Many biologists consider these migrating springbok herds the greatest concentration of large mammals ever recorded.

Nonetheless, by the end of the First World War, South Africa's springbok population had dwindled to a few scattered bands. While colonists certainly shot their share for subsistence (as did soldiers during the Boer War) and sometimes killed them in large numbers when they disrupted livestock grazing activities, bullets were not the proximate cause of this abrupt decline.

The rinderpest virus first appeared in southern Africa shortly before the springbok population began to crash. Although this epidemic disease of domestic livestock destroyed much of the region's cattle herd, authorities are still divided over its effect on springbok. On the other hand, the continued development of agriculture in historic springbok habitat, especially when it included extensive fencing, certainly proved disastrous. Springbok habitually undertook long, seasonal migrations in large herds, an activity termed *trekbokken*, in response to seasonal fluctuations in the availability of water and preferred food sources. Modern wire fences disrupted those crucial movement patterns, and large springbok populations could not survive.

Later in the twentieth century, populations of large mammals in southern Africa began to rebound much as they did in North America, at least in isolated areas. Colonial governments belatedly enacted game laws restricting the take of game animals by private citizens, and parcels of land owned and administered by these governments were set aside as refuges for wildlife. The boom in outdoor recreation that followed the end of the Second World War meant increased interest in safari hunting by visiting sportsmen of ordinary means, and wildlife on the hoof began to acquire its own intrinsic value. At the same time, Africa's indigenous population began to increase dramatically, causing more competition between wildlife and people for living space, and the post-colonial era eventually ushered in new political uncertainties, the collapse of many social institutions, and frequent armed conflict.

Since Africa is a huge, complex place, different approaches to wildlife management invariably arose in different nations. In what was formerly British East Africa, governments managed to set aside large tracts of land as undeveloped reserves and manage them for the benefit of both wildlife and the local economies, often with considerable success. In southern Africa, where colonial agricultural settlement had taken place much earlier and tracts of potential habitat had already been divided into smaller parcels, private ranches made the transition from raising livestock to raising wildlife—privately owned and managed, and generally confined by fencing.

Hunters played important roles in the execution and funding of both models. There were obvious advantages and disadvantages to each from the standpoint of all concerned: sportsmen, safari operators, local residents, and most importantly the wildlife itself. However much one might object to any given aspect of either approach, both provided wildlife with an outcome better than the prevailing alternative in many other parts of Africa: decimation in the face of political conflict and lawlessness.

That was the state of affairs when I made my first trip to Africa in 1993 and encountered a habitat project that managed to combine the best elements of these two models. Until it fell victim to political instability, it proved an unqualified success in the eyes of most knowledgeable observers, and it certainly benefited the populations of wildlife it supported. It also provided a sterling example of what can happen when conservationists of various backgrounds set aside their differences and work together for the good of wildlife.

The *lowveldt* country along the Save River in what is now southeastern Zimbabwe was historically good to wildlife, but not to the early European colonists who began to arrive there after the Boer War. Malaria and sleeping sickness kept them out of the Save Valley until the 1920s, when a few ranchers began to trickle in and establish large cattle operations. One early arrival was James Whitall, who established the Humani Ranch along the banks of the Save in the 1930s.

By the 1980s drought had ravaged the region for years and the area's once-lush forage base had begun to suffer from erosion and overgrazing by domestic livestock. A consortium of ranchers from the area decided that raising cattle was no longer an economically viable option for them or the land. Motivated by a combination of financial concerns and romanticism, they decided to get rid of the cows and replace them with the indigenous wildlife their cattle had displaced, with an eventual goal of making wildlife an economically viable alternative to livestock. Eventually, the owners of twenty-four contiguous ranches formed the Save Valley Conservancy (SVC) in 1991. One was the Humani Ranch, now operated by James Whitall's son, Roger. Incorporating some 3,200 square kilometers (1,235 square miles) of prime habitat, the SVC became the largest private game reserve on the continent.

While it's hard to imagine two-dozen fiercely independent Montana ranchers pooling their resources into a common entity, somehow their Zimbabwean counterparts did it. And they began to restore the land to its original wildlife potential with remarkable speed and efficiency, reintroducing game with surplus stock from other areas. Adaptive ungulates like kudu and bushbuck had hung on all along, but big game like rhino, buffalo, and elephant had long been eliminated and had to be replaced. Virtually all of the internal cattle fencing came down, allowing free movement of wildlife within the reserve. With the habitat recovering rapidly from decades of overgrazing, the new animals thrived upon arrival and rapidly began to reproduce.

Of course, all this took money. Fortunately, the Save Valley holds some of the best rhino habitat in the world, and the SVC partnered with the World Wildlife Fund to provide safe haven for the black rhino. (Unlike the white rhino, the black rhino is critically endangered as a result of commercial poaching for its horns, which fetch huge sums in the illegal market for dagger handles and traditional Asian medicines.) By the end of the decade, half the black rhinos in Zimbabwe were living in the SVC.

Individual ranchers still maintained control over commercial enterprise within their boundaries, and a few offered eco-tourism and photographic safaris. Even more focused on carefully regulated hunting; one of them was Roger Whitall. Sportsmen soon became by far the largest source of funding for the conservancy.

I visited the Humani Ranch three times between 1993 and 2000. Hunting with a traditional longbow, I didn't kill much—a bushbuck, a few bushpigs and impala—which emphasizes an important point in itself: Sportsmen contributing to wildlife do not necessarily ask much in return. The lush habitat was remarkable to begin with, and I watched it improve steadily each time I returned. Survivor species—kudu, bushbuck, bushpigs—predominated at first, but over the course of the years I watched the remarkable rebound of a host of others, including elephant, eland, sable, waterbuck, wildebeest, and buffalo. Despite some inevitable back-and-forth between hunting and non-hunting interests, potential conflicts generally resolved smoothly. The initial conservation emphasis fell upon big game for one simple reason: That's what paid the bills. But, as in our own country, restoring game means restoring habitat, which benefits the entire ecosystem. Most non-hunting visitors to the SVC readily accepted that fact.

The Humani Ranch included areas dedicated to hunting with firearms as well as areas reserved for bows and cameras, but it also had room for the Hippo Lady: Karen Paolillo, who personally tended the imperiled local hippo population through years of drought and founded the Turgwe River Hippo Trust in 1994.

Dig deep enough anywhere in Africa, and you'll come up against a recurring problem in wildlife management. In Africa, undisturbed living space is almost always the rate-limiting step in the reaction leading to wildlife recovery. Space for wildlife must come at the expense of space for something else. My first visit to the SVC illustrated the issue dramatically. The conservancy still maintained external fencing as required by law, to prevent the potential spread of hoof-and-mouth disease from buffalo and wildebeest to domestic livestock outside the SVC. Inside the fence, the habitat was lush and pristine; outside, domestic goats had grazed the ground cover down to dirt. Anyone involved in African wildlife conservation will have to face these contrasts, whether they hunt or not. The SVC addressed the matter proactively by forming the Save Valley Conservancy Trust, an entity that partnered with residents of villages outside the conservancy's borders to allow them economic development opportunities, access to communal resources within the SVC, and a share of SVC income. Furthermore, activities within the SVC funded by scarce hard currency (largely derived from hunting) quickly created a wealth of good jobs.

Workers inside the SVC enjoyed ample supplies of food, clothing, and shelter as well as steady wages that were quite high by regional standards. Their children attended well-run schools, and they had access to basic medical care. Taken out of context this doesn't sound like much, but anyone who considers these benefits patronizing cannot have spent much time in rural Africa. At one point the government polled the black population of the SVC, anticipating a vote of no confidence in the private land ownership model that would pave the way for a takeover. Resident workers voted overwhelmingly to leave the SVC structure alone.

The vision that inspired the SVC accomplished a tremendous amount for both people and wildlife. I still consider it a model of cooperation among various wildlife groups, and note with interest the parallel evolution of the American Prairie Foundation in eastern Montana, which faced many of the same problems and independently came up with many of the same solutions half a world away.

A story like this deserves a happy ending, but the SVC doesn't have one, at least not as of yet. It frankly held out longer than I expected in the face of political violence inspired by the Mugabe government, but as of this writing, the walls have been breached. Much of the wildlife that people worked so hard to restore has fallen victim to snares, and much of the habitat inside the reserve now looks like the land just outside its boundaries. Two black rhinos were recently found poached for their horns. Large tracts of land have been taken over by "war veterans," many of whom had not yet been born at the time of the colonial independence struggle.

South African professional hunter Maurice Nichols, who is as familiar with the area and its wildlife as anyone, sounded a note of guarded optimism when I spoke to him recently: "All is not lost yet. The current government is under real threat, and the opposition has the support of the population. I feel change is imminent. I have hunted and explored most of Africa south of the Zambezi River and can honestly say that Humani Ranch and the surrounding area is not just the best hunting terrain and wildlife habitat I have found but, with its tremendous biodiversity, one of the most fascinating and beautiful places on the planet." The story of Zimbabwe's descent into chaos isn't over, but, like Nichols, I can only hope that the SVC doesn't become reduced to an interesting footnote in the history of wildlife conservation.

Asia

I grew up in a family of hunters and anglers. When I was very young, my friends' parents read them *Winnie the Pooh* or *The Wind in the Willows* before they went to bed at night, while my own father read me stories from Colonel Jim Corbett's *Maneaters of India*. (I realize that I've just dated myself badly by admitting that I grew up when parents still read *anything* to their kids rather than letting them pass out in front of their computer games.) I still regard Corbett's modest, unassuming chronicles of his efforts to protect the hill people of northern India, where he lived and worked as a civil servant, from predatory tigers and leopards among the finest outdoor literature of all time. Corbett certainly had a profound effect on me. By the time I was six, he'd convinced me that I wanted to be a hunter, writer, and traveler when I grew up instead of a cowboy or a fireman. So far, so good.

It took me a while to get to Asia, but I finally made it, to the Soviet Far East in 1990, just as the Soviet Union, with which we'd waged cold war throughout my lifetime, teetered on the verge of collapse. Two close friends from Alaska, Anchorage businessmen and outdoorsmen Doug Borland and Ernie Holland, had been among the first Americans to travel there after the region's borders opened. Our mission at the time was to explore angling and bow hunting opportunities with an eye to developing potential outfitting joint ventures with the Russians, and over the course of the next two years, we experienced enough adventure in the bush to fuel a book of its own. We'll confine the discussion here to an examination of the Russian approach to wildlife in this uniquely remote setting during a time of profound political upheaval.

It didn't take long to recognize the complete absence of familiar wildlife management principles. We found essentially no rules governing the interactions between people and wild animals. Because of the miserable state of the Russian economy after decades of failed Communism, sport hunting and angling were virtually unknown, and the prevailing attitude toward fish and game seemed more reminiscent of colonial North America than anything we'd ever experienced.

We found out all about it on the first afternoon of a bow hunt for brown bears. Recognizing the culture gap from the start, we'd tried our best to discuss our own concepts of sportsmanship with our new Russian friends before we set out from our camp on a wilderness gravel bar. While the language barrier made a hard task even harder, we thought we'd made the important points to our Russian companions, a trio of sable trappers who were some of the toughest woodsmen I'd ever met.

Less than an hour up the salmon stream where the bears were feeding, principle encountered reality when we blundered into a sow and cubs. When the surprised cubs scooted up a nearby larch tree, the Russians promptly began shouting for me to shoot them. Unfortunately, I scarcely had time to savor the Teddy Roosevelt opportunity to decline as the sow burst out of the brush, mad as a hornet. Russians raised rifles; Americans tried to organize a retreat without killing any of the bears. Amazingly enough, we accomplished that at the expense of nothing but a few warning shots, at which point we retreated to camp to talk more about American concepts of sportsmanship.

It was not an easy discussion. Sergei, a remarkably capable backwoodsman with whom I eventually spent several enjoyable weeks in the bush, took off his shirt and counted the scars from the three serious bear maulings he'd survived. Andrei explained how the bears regularly destroyed the cabins they depended upon for their survival when they ran their trap lines in the winter. "The bears are our enemies here on the *taiga*," Sergei concluded. "They kill us and we kill them."

To complicate matters further, bear gallbladders, like many other exotic wildlife parts, had become extremely valuable commodities on the nearby Korean traditional medicine market, where they were processed into aphrodisiacs. (The subsequent development of Viagra may eventually prove to be the best thing that ever happened to a host of wild game species ranging from bears and tigers to rhinos.) One bear gallbladder was worth months of wages in hard currency to the Russians, a powerful incentive to kill in an economy teetering on the verge of collapse.

Despite all these considerations, the bear population seemed to be in excellent shape, with densities as high or higher than all but the very best brown bear habitat we knew in Alaska. The reason for this disconnection was readily apparent: We were traveling through largely inaccessible terrain that had seen almost no human development since V. K. Arseniev described it a century before in his classic chronicle *Dursu the Hunter*. But how would Russian bears, sheep, and moose fare in the face of the avalanche of societal change taking place in Moscow while we were tramping the *taiga* a dozen time zones away? We were the pioneers, but it was already just a matter of time until economic and political changes opened the backcountry to Russians and foreigners alike. Absent a sea change in attitude, we found it difficult to be optimistic. We also had to acknowledge that our own presence there had the potential to do as much harm as good.

Over the course of two seasons, we tried our best. We held countless campfire discussions (most admittedly fueled by ubiquitous Russian vodka) about American concepts of sportsmanship with our various Russian companions. On that count at least, we experienced considerable success, although I have no idea how far it extended beyond our immediate circle. By the end of our last expedition, the Russians were smiling when we passed up stalks on bears we didn't want to shoot instead of drawing down on them with their carbines.

But in hungry country, sportsmanship and a quarter will get you a cup of coffee and not much more. At some point, *not* shooting bears was going to have to make economic sense. We tried our best to explain that healthy, well-managed wildlife populations could translate into a sustainable resource good for steady jobs paying hard currency. That proved a far harder sell. After a lifetime of Communism, the Russians had no concept of basic free-market economic principles, including the value of investing for the future. (Though when the dams broke in Moscow, it didn't take them long to learn their own relentless brand of capitalism.) Furthermore, I found the Russians to be the most pessimistic people I'd ever met, admittedly with good reason. In town, when someone turned on a television, no one in the room expected it to work. In the bush, when we came across a remote body of water, the Russians always assumed it was devoid of fish. (I disproved this assumption time and again with my fly rod, to the delight of all at the next meal.) In this context, the notion that a live animal tomorrow might be worth more than a dead one today becomes extremely difficult to grasp.

Did our counsel have any impact on the future of wildlife in the area we visited? Frankly, I don't know. For a variety of complex reasons, the situation on the ground became untenable for us and we never went back. As much as I'd love to hear from the friends we made there, communications are essentially impossible. The area certainly has opened up to international sport hunting. Unfortunately, anecdotal reports I've received from the field include numerous disappointing examples of unfortunate practices.

Doug Borland's subsequent experiences elsewhere in Russia lend credence to this pessimistic assessment. At the time when we were thrashing around with the bears in the Far East, it was becoming apparent to insiders that the Kola Peninsula offered the greatest undiscovered Atlantic salmon fishing in the world. Married to a Russian cardiologist by this time, Doug set out to explore the possibilities of establishing a fly-fishing lodge as a Russian-American joint venture. The salmon runs exceeded his expectations—unfortunately, so did the local appetite for fish soup.

Doug and his wife, Olga, were hardly naive. Recognizing the importance of enlisting local support for the project from the start, they hired guides and paid them well from revenues derived from the first exploratory bookings. They were not competing economically with established commercial fisheries interests, since the infrastructure couldn't get fresh fish to market in distant population centers. (We'd encountered the same phenomenon in the Russian Far East, where Pacific salmon runs as rich as Alaska's went unharvested for the same reason.) But despite the obvious (to us) economic benefits of developing a managed sport fishery in a remote, economically depressed area, the locals just couldn't see past dinner, never mind the fact that boiling wild Atlantic salmon with onions is the culinary equivalent of grinding prime beef tenderloin into hot dogs. By day, everyone operated in fraternal agreement; by night, the nets went into the river. After a series of increasingly tense confrontations, the Borlands gave up, to the ultimate detriment of both the fish and the people who lived next to them.

This brief segment on hunting and wildlife in Asia warrants a final tip of the hat to the individual who influenced me so much as a child and who still remains an important if underappreciated example of the sportsman-conservationist: Jim Corbett.

Market-driven technology seems determined to replace skill and knowledge in the field these days, to the shame of those hunters and anglers who allow it. In contrast, Corbett still represents my ideal of the consummate hunter: a woodsman and naturalist rather than merely someone who shoots. As a writer, he offers much to admire. The dangerous game genre is perhaps the trickiest of all outdoor sporting literature, thanks to the ease with which it invites hyperbole and self-promotion. Several of its modern practitioners are all but unreadable. Solid pros like Hemingway and Ruark blew it not infrequently, and even Teddy Roosevelt's *African Game Trails* grows tedious in places despite the value of its descriptions of African wildlife a century ago and its insights into Roosevelt's character. But Corbett never forgot the identity of each story's true, if tragically flawed, hero. It wasn't about Corbett; it was about the tiger.

Corbett illustrates an interesting take on one of North American wildlife management's basic principles: Wildlife should not be killed without a valid reason. If there is a better justification than the legitimate use of wildlife for food, Corbett found it. At least during the long, latter part of his hunting career, he only killed known man-eaters, exposing himself to extremes of risk none of us will ever know in the field. It's hard for us today to fathom the kind of terror a man-eating great cat could generate among an unarmed rural populace in the remote hill country of northern India a century ago. Some of the tigers and leopards Corbett tracked down killed hundreds of defenseless villagers during their careers. Corbett left the rest of them alone.

All of this took place before Gandhi led India out of colonialism. Corbett's genuine regard for the villagers to whose aid he came was way ahead of its time. So was his regard for the tigers. He was among the first to recognize and call attention to the impending crisis the great cats would inevitably face as more and more humans intruded upon more and more of their habitat. Corbett played important roles in forming the Association for the Preservation of Game in the United Provinces and the All-India Conference for the Preservation of Wildlife. In 1957 India's first national park (originally founded in the Kumaon Hills as the Hailey National Park in 1934) was renamed in Corbett's honor, and in 1968 one of the five remaining subspecies of tigers was renamed *Panther tigris corbetti*.

While the very idea of naming a tiger and a national park dedicated to the preservation of tiger habitat after one of the most accomplished tiger hunters of all time may seem paradoxical at first, it should come as no surprise to anyone familiar with the symbiotic link between sportsmen and conservation. Few exemplify that concept at its best like Jim Corbett.

This survey of issues facing sportsmen and wildlife in other nations is admittedly arbitrary. Wildlife policies and practices elsewhere often differ as much from each other as they do from our own, which makes generalization difficult. But outdoor travel around the world—in Latin American and the Pacific in addition to Asia and Africa—has allowed me to identify certain principles when comparing our own model to those in other nations.

Wildlife is often the first casualty of political conflict. Long on wildlife but short on political security, Africa illustrates this point dramatically, and not just in Zimbabwe. Armed conflicts are endemic throughout Africa, and the status of wildlife seems to vary directly with the degree of security available. In developing countries, political stability can be as important as habitat to the future of wildlife.

Managing wildlife by rule of law requires appropriate will and means. In functional states, applying the legal system to effective wildlife management, as we do here, is fairly easy. This is not true in nations that cannot provide basic security for their own citizens, let alone their wildlife. Under these circumstances, privatization of wildlife—as inappropriate as that practice is in North America—may be preferable to other alternatives.

In developing nations, wildlife will have to pay its own way. In much of the world, caring for wildlife for its own sake is an unaffordable luxury that will always take a backseat to the immediate necessities of human survival. North American wildlife management principles arose in nations fortunate enough to enjoy a relative abundance of two often-scarce resources: money and large tracts of unpopulated land suitable for wildlife habitat. Elsewhere, wildlife often exists in direct competition with local means of livelihood. In such circumstances, healthy populations of wildlife have to acquire value in order to survive. The devil may be in the details, but as long as cattle are worth more than kudu, habitat will contain cows rather than the wildlife that rightfully belongs there.

Wildlife needs to be valuable to the people on the ground. Poverty, like conflict, is inherently an enemy of wildlife. It's difficult to combat poaching when the immediate alternative is a hungry family. No matter what deals are struck in urban capitals, wildlife will always lose unless its welfare coincides with the interests of its immediate human neighbors. Accomplishing this goal almost always requires foresight and skilled communications. At their best, hunters and anglers can play a critical role in this process.

In the long term, neither sport nor wildlife will thrive if they benefit the social elite exclusively. This principle is best illustrated by its violation in other nations—just ask the British gentry how they enjoyed their foxhunting season last year.

As a writer, I've been fortunate enough to enjoy abundant opportunities to travel to wild places throughout the world, learning firsthand about exotic wildlife, other cultures, and the way the two interact. I've seen plenty to emulate in the process. The original Save River Conservancy, for example, could serve as a valuable model for the American Prairie Foundation's ambitious habitat project in eastern Montana. And I'd love to see all American guides and outfitters held to something approaching the original standards for Zimbabwean professional hunters. (Alaska makes the best attempt of all the states, but even Alaskan guides—of which I'm one myself—would have a long way to go.)

Nonetheless, I seldom return from an overseas expedition without a heightened appreciation of how good both sportsmen and wildlife have it here at home.

FIERCE GREEN FIRE

While sportsmen have certainly made positive contributions to the preservation of wildlife and their habitat,
it would be naive to assume that any group has always
acted with the best intentions toward our wild resources, sportsmen included. No issue illustrates this point like the history of
our treatment of large predators, a matter in which sportsmen
have mirrored the frequently confused and misguided attitudes
of society at large.

Healthy populations of bears, cougars, and wolves once
inhabited virtually all of the contiguous states, and early colonists
encountered them in abundance along the eastern seaboard. By
the time the bison was making its last stand in Yellowstone at
the beginning of the twentieth century, most large predators had
been extirpated east of the Mississippi except for scattered, isolated populations in a dwindling amount of suitable habitat, and
public policy throughout much of the West seemed intent upon
extending their elimination all the way to the Pacific.

A qualitative change in attitude has significantly reversed that
trend over the last several decades (with a few notable exceptions),
and predator numbers have rebounded across much of their original range. While sportsmen were not the prime cause of those
near-catastrophic population declines, they must shoulder part
of the blame. Similarly, while they may not have been the prime
agent in their recovery, sportsmen deserve some of the credit.
Analysis of this confusing record provides useful insight into the
future of large predators and sportsmen alike.

Early colonists found the ubiquitous American black bear—
a new species to them—an important resource. Absent modern
prejudices against eating bear meat (an unfortunate bias, as anyone

who has eaten a bear from a fall berry patch knows), they valued bear as a food source. Hides were also prized for the insulation they provided as blankets, and bear fat was valuable as a leather conditioner, waterproofing agent, and calorie-rich food supplement. Early settlers hunted bears enthusiastically if inefficiently, with negligible impact upon their populations.

The eventual establishment of livestock rearing and agriculture on a larger scale ushered in a new attitude toward bears, which raided crops and found domesticated animals easy prey. Growing numbers of colonial livestock also drew the attention of wolves and cougars. In contrast to the black bear, neither of these species ever received attention as a subsistence quarry, so it was even easier to rationalize formal attempts to eradicate them.

The concept of bounties on predatory animals crossed the Atlantic with the colonists. Sweden created bounties on bears in 1647 and maintained them until 1893. Finland enacted bounties on nearly two-dozen species of predators of all kinds the same year as its Scandinavian neighbor, and remarkably kept them on the books until 1975. Given the us-versus-them attitude ascendant in the rapidly expanding colonies toward everything from wildlife to Native Americans, it was only a matter of time until a bounty system arose here.

Massachusetts led the way, establishing bounties on wolves in the 1600s. (The last wolf in Massachusetts was killed in 1837.) By the Revolutionary War, Virginia had established a bounty on bears; in one county, it remained in effect until 1977. Eventually, bounties on large predators became nearly ubiquitous throughout the East, though their timing varied from colony to colony and eventually from state to state.

The bounty-hunting era initiated a qualitative change in human impact on predator populations. Early colonial subsistence hunters, who needed not just a dead bear but one that could be salvaged promptly for utilization, relied on firearms as their principle means of take. Hunting with primitive weapons, they originally lacked the ability to kill any large animal species in biologically significant numbers. Bounty hunters suffered no such constraints, as they only needed to provide evidence of a dead predator to claim their reward. Income from bounties allowed them the means to maintain trained hound packs, and they also employed a variety of traps, snares, and baited hooks. As in the case of commercial bison hunters in the century that followed, cash turned Revolutionary-era hunters into efficient killers.

While such deliberate destruction of large animals by human means arouses immediate emotional response among those who value wildlife (including hunters), it was certainly not the only, or even the most significant, cause of predator extirpation in the eastern United States. As a group, large predators exhibit low reproductive efficiency, require large home ranges, and demonstrate low population densities even under the best habitat conditions. They tolerate human presence poorly and require large parcels of security habitat to thrive. All these factors leave them particularly vulnerable to habitat degradation by human expansion and development of the very kind at which American settlers excelled. Clearing forests and draining swamps may not sound as lethal as a hunter's bullet, at least in its immediate intent. Nonetheless, these activities ultimately contributed more to the elimination of large predators in the East than all hunters—subsistence, bounty, and sport—combined.

The pattern of human interactions with large predators in the West mirrored its history in the East, with several qualifications. Because the West was settled so much later, a time lag occurred, and by the time western wolves, bears, and lions first encountered white men with guns, their counterparts had already been eliminated from much of the East. Since ranching was such an important part of the western economy, stockmen's attitudes toward predators tended to dominate state policy, as it does in many parts of the West today. And because this area contained most of the suitable large predator habitat left in the contiguous states, policy toward predators remained an important and controversial issue in the West long after wolves and lions had been extirpated from the East.

Because of an abundance of wild ungulates as a ready food source, bears—black and grizzly—were never an important subsistence staple for early western pioneers. Nonetheless, the plains grizzly that Lewis and Clark described so memorably was rapidly eliminated from the open terrain of the upper Midwest through isolated encounters between bears and rifles, reflecting the bears' belligerent nature and the fear it aroused among early settlers.

Organized efforts at predator eradication did not arise until the arrival of large numbers of domestic livestock. This 1849 Oregon statute is representative of what followed:

> Be it enacted by the Legislative Assembly of the Territory
> of Oregon; that there shall be paid out of the county
> treasury of the proper county on the order of the county
> commissioners to any person who shall . . . present to said
> court, the scalp of any panther, tiger, cougar, lynx, wild-cat,
> large-wolf, or prairie wolf and declare under oath that the
> animal from which the said scalp was taken was killed in
> the said county; when the same is presented, the following
> premiums shall be awarded; viz for each panther, the sum
> of three dollars; for each tiger, the sum of three dollars; for
> each cougar, the sum of three dollars; for each lynx, the sum
> of three dollars; for each wild-cat, the sum of one dollar; for
> each large-wolf, the sum of three dollars, for each prairie
> wolf, the sum of one dollar and fifty cents.

Politicians evidently had as much difficulty with wildlife biology then as they do now. They considered the panther and the cougar two separate species, and the biological source of the Oregon Territory's perceived "tiger" problem remains a mystery.

Similar predator-control measures soon arose elsewhere around the West. Although the "golden bear" figured prominently in early California lore and appears on the state flag, the state offered a $10 bounty on grizzlies for years. Washington offered a bounty on cougars from 1904 to 1961. A bounty on wolves was in effect in Montana from 1884 to 1933; the state paid a high of 4,416 wolf bounties in 1903.

While much of the political motivation for the bounty system arose from the livestock industry, sportsmen were hardly innocent bystanders. Colorado authorized a cougar bounty shortly after statehood, but that evidently wasn't enough for some. The *Denver Post* offered its own private $25 reward for dead cougars as rationalized in this vintage editorial: "It is the duty of every true Coloradan to do his best to rid the state of these beasts which kill so much game. By no other means than the hunting out of the mountain lion and killing them can the game be protected." (Colorado's lion bounty was revoked in 1965, with the support of the *Denver Post*.)

As the *Post*'s original editorial position demonstrates, many sportsmen of the time viewed large predators primarily as a source of competition for what was by then a dwindling supply of game animals. While habitat loss to development and unregulated subsistence and market hunting were the primary factors in that decline, predators made a convenient scapegoat, as they do in some circles today. Though some early twentieth-century hunters regarded large predators as legitimate quarry and accorded them a measure of respect, prevailing attitudes reflected the quintessentially American civilization-versus-nature ethic Ahab displayed in *Moby Dick*.

As Paul Schullery reports in *The Bear Hunter's Century*, Ben Lilly, arguably the most effective and relentless predator hunter the West ever produced, seems to have had a positively visceral loathing for his quarry. And sportsman William Hornaday exemplified this contemporary attitude in a 1914 presentation at Yale (in his capacity as president of the Permanent Wildlife Protection Agency, no less): "The eradication of the puma from certain districts it now infests to a deplorable extent is a task of immediate urgency . . . We consider firearms, dogs, traps, and strychnine thoroughly legitimate weapons of destruction for such animals, no half way measure will suffice."

Against the background of such an ethic, Theodore Roosevelt's well-publicized decision to pass up the shot at his "Teddy Bear" seems all the more enlightened.

Change came during the twentieth century, albeit slowly, as the eventual elimination of the bounty system on large predators demonstrates. The evolution of Aldo Leopold's views on the subject offers a telling illustration. In the early days of his field career, Leopold's attitude toward predators was nearly as virulent as Hornaday's. Then, on a Forest Service assignment in the Southwest in 1909, he experienced an epiphany of sorts during a lethal wolf encounter, as he later recounted in *A Sand County Almanac*:

> In those days we had never heard of passing up a chance to
> kill a wolf. In a second we were pumping lead into the pack,
> but with more excitement than accuracy: how to aim a steep
> downhill shot is always confusing. When our rifles were
> empty, the old wolf was down and a pup was dragging a leg
> into impassable slide rocks.
>
> We reached the old wolf in time to see the fierce green
> fire dying in her eyes. I realized then, and have known
> ever since, that there was something new to me in those
> eyes—something known only to her and the mountain. I was
> young then, and full of trigger-itch; I thought that because
> fewer wolves meant more deer, that no wolves would mean a
> hunter's paradise. But after seeing the green fire die, I sensed
> that neither the wolf nor the mountain agreed with this view.

This passage has been widely cited out of context to suggest that the event left Leopold with an antipathy toward hunting in general. This was certainly not the case, as he remained an ardent outdoorsman and hunter throughout his life. But the angst all responsible hunters feel at some level when they kill an animal certainly made him rethink the prevailing attitudes toward predators that he once shared.

In fact, Leopold's eventual enlightened attitude toward predators owed more to the emerging science of wildlife biology, which he pioneered, than to his eloquently expressed regret at the death of an individual wolf. Not long after the extinction of that "fierce green fire," ruthlessly effective predator control on Arizona's Kaibab Plateau resulted in an explosion in mule deer numbers, to the transient delight of hunters. But the erupting deer population soon overgrazed its dry, fragile habitat. The deer herd crashed, and the damage their excess numbers had done to the ecosystem proved so severe that the land and the game it once supported did not recover for decades.

Leopold was too keen an observer to ignore the lessons such experiences taught. In 1935 he wrote: "By killing off all species having predatory tendencies we may have been doing a greater damage to our game species than ever did the predators." Modern scientific consensus suggests he was right, although that opinion has not been universally accepted, as Alaska's recent campaign against wolves and bears in an attempt to boost moose populations demonstrates.

By the mid to late twentieth century, the bounty system on large predators had largely been dismantled, although the USDA Wildlife Service continues to "control" predators, including cougars, wolves, and bears, at the behest of agricultural interests. (Thousands of representatives of a dozen different species were eliminated in Montana in fiscal year 2007.) Populations recovered substantially in most states commensurate with the animals' change in status from varmint to game species, two developments interrelated in their cause and effect. Hunters' attitudes in general toward bears and lions mirrored the evolution in Leopold's thinking. And sportsmen did play a role in changing the policy approach to those species, although sometimes without the enthusiasm the issue warranted.

But the issue remains contentious, and likely always will. In *Monster of God*, his excellent study of the historical, cultural, and biological relationship between people and large predators, David Quammen documents the near-mythical status humans have always accorded wild animals sufficiently large and dangerous to harm them, and the unease that capacity has aroused in virtually every human society that has shared living space with such creatures. That unease has not dissipated even in the era of modern firearms, as anyone who has spent time in wilderness grizzly country likely knows.

Even when they're not eating us (lest I stand accused of hyperbole, note that several hundred people are still killed and eaten by lions every year in East Africa), the stature these animals hold in the human imagination—an odd amalgam of fear and loathing flavored with admiration and respect—makes them lightning rods for animosity out of all proportion to their actual impact. Studies show that fewer than 5 percent of all livestock losses on open western rangelands are due to predators, yet stockmen seem to worry about wolves and cougars more than all other threats to their sheep and cattle combined. And nine out of ten Montana hunters I know who didn't fill an elk tag last year blame reintroduced wolves for their failure, even though most of them rarely killed elk when Montana wolves were nothing but a memory.

What does this conflicted history mean for wildlife today and the future of hunting? The highly controversial wolf reintroduction program in the Greater Yellowstone Ecosystem offers an illustrative example.

The last native wolf in Yellowstone National Park was killed in 1926. Once sport hunting was permanently banned within the park, the Yellowstone elk herd, essentially free of all predatory pressure, began to expand unchecked, to the detriment of the habitat and the concern of many biologists. A rapidly increasing bison population eventually contributed to the problem and aroused unique concerns of its own when the animals were shown to harbor brucellosis, a potential threat to the cattle industry outside the park.

In 1973 the gray wolf was listed as endangered under the Endangered Species Act (ESA). In 1993 the U.S. Fish and Wildlife Service (USFWS) released its final draft Environmental Impact Statement (EIS) for a proposed wolf recovery program, under mandate from Congress. In 1995 and 1996, sixty-six transplanted Canadian wolves were released in Yellowstone and another thirty-five in Idaho, initiating what will likely be the most contentious wildlife issue the region will see in our times.

A basic cultural dilemma plagued the program from the start. Most proponents of wolf reintroduction lived in distant, urban parts of the country and brought numerous alien values to the table (when they came to the table at all). Residents of the Mountain West, on the other hand, are notoriously resistant to outsiders telling them what to do. It was clear to me from the start that the firestorm of controversy that wolf recovery initiated was about more than wolves.

Naturally enough, local ranchers concerned about their livestock headed the initial opposition to wolf reintroduction. In an effort to address these concerns, Defenders of Wildlife offered to reimburse ranchers at fair market value rates for livestock lost to wolves. While they had paid out some $42,000 in compensation by 1997, the program was plagued by the inherent difficulty of confirming wolf kills, and most area ranchers found it unsatisfactory. Prevented by law from killing wolves even if they were caught in the act of killing livestock, ranchers' resentment rose steadily.

While few local hunters expressed enthusiasm for wolf recovery, their initial opposition was relatively timid compared to the ranchers'. However, hopes that wolves would significantly reduce Yellowstone's unsustainable bison population soon proved unfounded. The wolves were interested in elk, and elk numbers began to decline. By how much? Initial estimates from authoritative sources in the USFWS suggested 5 percent, but by 2005 state biologists had documented a ten-year decline in the Yellowstone elk herd from seventeen thousand to eight thousand. Of further concern to hunters, wolves seemed to prey selectively on large, mature bulls, which are isolated and weakened during the winter following the rut.

Wolves may have been just partly to blame for the population drop. A hard winter in 1997 killed a lot of game, and the entire region suffered through several years of drought. But by this time opinions had become so polarized that most hunters rejected all such alternative explanations for what they were observing in the field. The area's human elk harvest decreased, local outfitters went out of business, and despite the opinions of a few hunters willing to trade some elk for an opportunity to hear wolves howl at night, sporting interests generally became aligned with the ranchers.

Meanwhile, a biological success story was in progress, at least for those who could distance themselves from the increasingly bitter politics. The initial recovery goal called for thirty independent wolf packs; by 2004 there were seventy-one. Interior Secretary Gale Norton declared the wolf recovered and invited the states to assume their management. Despite the ruminations of federal conspiracy theorists, Ed Bangs, the USFWS Wolf Recovery team leader and an old bow hunting friend from our days together in the same Alaska town, had assured me of this intention all along.

By this point, the only clear winners in addition to the wolves were the lawyers (and I shall resist any temptation to posit kinship). Seldom in the history of wildlife politics have so many suits been filed by so many over so little. In 1994, prior to the first wolf release, the Wyoming Farm Bureau and a coalition of environmental groups *both* sued in federal court to overturn the introduced wolf population's initial designation as "experimental and non-essential" under the ESA. Wolf recovery advocates wanted the "non-essential" designation stricken, while the ranch group argued that unofficial wolf sightings in the area confirmed a naturally occurring wolf population that could be threatened by introduced wolves from Canada. (The suits were dismissed.) The pace of litigation continues to this day as wolf advocates challenge the recent federal decision to delist in court despite clear evidence that the program has vastly exceeded its biological goals.

To what should be no one's surprise, the delisting process has not gone easily. In order for the USFWS to relinquish control of wolf management as both state and federal agencies wanted all along, each of the three states in the recovery area—Montana, Idaho, and Wyoming—needed to present an acceptable management plan. Montana and Idaho did, but, in an act of political posturing to its rabidly anti-wolf constituents, Wyoming's initial proposed management plan boiled down to *shoot them all*. Not surprisingly, that idea did not pass federal muster, leading to a four-year (and still ongoing) delay during which the states could not manage wolves, ranchers could not protect their livestock, hunters could not hunt surplus wolves, and the wolf population continued to soar beyond recovery goals. Politicians, it appears, haven't learned much since the 1846 Oregon Territorial legislature declared war on tigers.

The relationship among wolves, ranchers, "environmentalists" (for want of a better term), and sportsmen in the Greater Yellowstone area remains contentious and confusing. Can any lessons be drawn from all the acrimony that might be instructive for the future of wildlife and hunting?

I would first note the triumph of emotionalism over science in this controversy, and its adverse effect on outcome. As in Middle Eastern politics, rational discussion and willingness to compromise remain conspicuous by their absence. Reading a decade's worth of literature on the wolf recovery project creates the impression of two different events being described by people speaking two different languages. Opinions seem divided into two different camps: worship the wolves or kill them all. As usual when analyzing such highly polarized positions, the truth almost certainly lies somewhere between, yet it is remarkably hard to find any expression of the middle ground. While large predators seem almost uniquely capable of arousing this kind of emotionally charged response to wildlife, this is obviously not the way to solve complex management problems. As Utah State University wildlife ecologist Charles Kay observed in an attempt to establish the missing middle ground: "I am committed neither to having wolves in the West nor to keeping them out. I am committed though to science used responsibly in policy debates, something I have not yet seen in wolf recovery."

Second, our collective fascination with the wolf pro and con illustrates the natural human tendency to focus attention on dramatic, "sexy" species at the expense of what really matters to wildlife: Leopold's quartet of clean air, clean water, ample food, and a place to live, conveniently reduced in shorthand to *habitat*. What really matters isn't the fate of the individual grizzly bear, but the well-being of the white bark pine or red salmon upon which the entire population of bears depends for ongoing survival. Yet discussion of such apparently mundane but ultimately critical matters remains remarkably absent from both sides of the wolf reintroduction controversy. Focusing attention one way or the other on charismatic species atop the food chain at the expense of less compelling but fundamentally more important habitat issues does not bode well for the future of wildlife.

Finally, all parties to the dispute made basic errors in political judgment. Recovery activists showed a remarkable lack of appreciation for western sensibilities from the start. An attempt to appreciate local concerns and accommodate them within reason might well have avoided long rounds of expensive litigation and left the wolf a more secure environment in the long run. Recovery advocates' belligerence stands in marked contrast to the approach of the American Prairie Foundation, which made an impressive effort to respond to local concerns *before* they went to work on the ground. The cooperation they earned serves them well to this day. On the other hand, by the year 2000 it should have been obvious to local ranchers and hunters that the wolf reintroduction was a federally mandated *fait accompli* whether they liked it or not. Political posturing from that point on has simply delayed the transfer of wolf management to the states, where it belongs. Surely we can do better in the future.

My personal views on the wolf recovery program could draw ire from both sides of the aisle. I admire wolves, appreciate their role in the ecosystem, and have enjoyed their presence on many wilderness excursions in the North. However, given the chance, I would have voted reluctantly against wolf reintroduction for four reasons, one petty and three more substantial, none having anything to do with the wolves' impact on elk and other game animals.

Like most Montanans, I don't like urban outsiders running roughshod over local sensibilities. (That's the petty concern.) Second, adjacent human development, although limited by modern standards, has made Greater Yellowstone unsuitable wolf habitat because of the inevitability of adverse encounters between livestock and wolves. The future of the species will be determined in large reaches of remote habitat in Alaska and northern Canada, and that's where preservation efforts should be directed. Third, human and financial resources (estimated recovery costs range from $200,000 to $1,000,000 per wolf) could have been used more wisely to benefit wildlife in other ways. Fourth, the acrimony wolf reintroduction inevitably generated has not been worth the political price to hunters, ranchers, or wildlife.

Sportsmen's attitudes toward large predators have often reflected the antipathy of society at large, and hunters have sometimes supported the elimination of predators as competitors for wild game resources despite the lack of science supporting such policies. However, they also played a significant role in the restoration of their numbers in the late twentieth century, particularly in the case of bears and cougars, as they became appreciated as quarry. Some of this effect was indirect: Lobbying for the creation of large areas of wild habitat protected from development created just the kind of security habitat large predators require.

But as they recognized the value of predators as game animals in their own right, sportsmen also began to work directly on their behalf. Alaska guides were instrumental in changing the status of the state's brown/grizzly bears from varmint to carefully managed resource. Of course, they were motivated by economic self-interest, but anyone familiar with old-time bear guides like Hal Waugh, Bill Pinnell, and Morris Talifson recognizes the genuine regard they felt for these animals. And today, as the State of Alaska continues a highly controversial predator-control program intended to address a decline in moose and caribou numbers and their subsequent lack of availability to hunters, sportsmen's groups like Backcountry Hunters and Anglers have taken principled positions against these measures.

Which leads to just the kind of middle ground so conspicuously absent from the wolf recovery debate . . . As I've argued in print before (*Big Sky Journal,* 2001), a logical model for the management of bears, wolves, and cougars already exists: Treat them as big game animals. We've already noted the temporal coincidence of large predator recovery and their attainment of game animal status in areas from which they had once been nearly or completely extirpated. While it might seem that hunting seasons were established on these animals because their numbers had recovered, the converse is true as well: According them game animal status instead of treating them as vermin, as Hornaday once advocated, allowed state wildlife agencies to afford them the same kind of protection available to traditional game species such as deer and elk and manage them according to scientific principles instead of emotionalism, which historically seldom worked in predators' favor. And, as always, the more people who have a vested interest in wildlife of any kind, the more likely it is to thrive.

While the predator-as-game-animal model makes sense as a matter of policy and biology, sportsmen can improve upon it by reexamining some of their traditional practices in the field, as they have already started to do in some cases. Studies consistently show that the non-hunting public is more likely to approve of hunting when hunters eat what they shoot and less likely when an animal is killed solely for the sake of a "trophy," as is often the case when predators are the quarry. Our subsistence-hunting colonial predecessors knew better. Montana and Alaska have both recently passed meat salvage regulations for bears (Alaska's is seasonal and does not apply to grizzlies), steps that will clearly increase the acceptability of bear hunting in the public eye. The failure to enact similar statutes with regard to cougars is unfortunate in light of the misguided opposition to lion hunting that has led to biologically unjustified restrictions or outright bans on the practice in several western states. Our cultural biases against eating cats are especially ironic, since cougar is actually one of the best-tasting wild game meats I know.

In contrast to their consistent advocacy on behalf of species as diverse as elk and waterfowl, sportsmen have logged a checkered record with regard to large predators. We can do better, and we need to. In moments of uncertainty it is always helpful to return to fixed principles. One of the seven cornerstones of the North American Model of Wildlife Conservation reminds us that wildlife should not be killed without a valid reason. Perhaps it is time to agree that killing one variety of animal solely for the presumed (but hardly proven) benefit of more "desirable" species does not fulfill the criterion of validity. The 80 percent of voting Americans who remain uncommitted about hunting but who will determine its future will appreciate the change. So, in the long run, will sportsmen and wildlife.

PART THREE

An Eye to the Future

THE NORTH AMERICAN
WILDLIFE CONSERVATION MODEL

As hunting, fishing, and wildlife itself face an uncertain future, it will be more important than ever to identify guiding principles to help navigate the challenging times ahead. North American sportsmen take a lot of assumptions for granted. Even as state wildlife regulations grow steadily more complex, we know without being told that certain things just aren't done in the field or on the stream, and we know that other things are mandatory. We know that there are open seasons and closed seasons and bag limits, and we know that all wildlife belongs to the public—at least in theory. One doesn't begin to realize how arbitrary these many givens really are without extensive travel and immersion in other models of wildlife management.

As I spent more time in other hunting cultures, I tried to define the principles that made North American hunting and wildlife management so unique, only to discover that I was reinventing the wheel. That task had already been done for me. In the 1990s writers working with the Wildlife Society formulated a group of concepts into what eventually became known as the North American Wildlife Conservation Model (NAWCM). Researching this chapter, I became frustrated by my inability to identify the exact moment at which someone gave what turned out to be an enduring idea its name, or the identity of the first person to use the term. At least I'm in good company on that point. Two of the NAWCM's most articulate proponents—wildlife biologist Valerius Geist, Professor Emeritus of Environmental Science at the University of Calgary, and Jim Posewitz, of the Orion Institute in Helena, Montana—can't remember the details either. Since no one in the field has ever worried much about taking credit for ideas, it probably doesn't matter.

Broken down into seven core principles, the NAWCM is remarkably easy to understand:

Wildlife is a public resource. This principle dates all the way back to Roman law, which acknowledged the concept of a class of property that no one could own privately but was held in common for use by all (*res communis*). Roman codes included wildlife in this category. Ownership of a wild animal only occurred when someone physically possessed it, as when an animal was killed for food. The Magna Carta introduced this principle to English law by making wildlife the property of the king, to be held in trust for the people.

Nonetheless, American colonists arriving in the New World from England left behind a system in which wildlife functionally belonged to the wealthy and powerful and was managed for their exclusive benefit despite this provision. Natural resentment of such exclusivity complicated early attempts at organized wildlife management in America. A largely unregulated free-for-all system sufficed until increasing settlement engendered conflicts that required the courts to rule on matters of wildlife ownership. In the landmark 1842 decision *Martin v. Waddell,* the Supreme Court held that the State of New Jersey, and not the private landowner who filed suit, owned the riparian zone along the Raritan River, including its wildlife. In 1896 the court upheld that principle in *Geer v. Connecticut,* when Justice Edward White wrote for the majority that the states had the "right to control and regulate the common property in game as a trust for the benefit of the people."

Obvious as this may seem to us, it is by no means a universal principle. I have hunted in some countries in which game belongs to the owner of the land it occupies, and others in which game belongs to whoever can get to it first.

Wildlife should not be bought or sold. This principle acknowledges the tremendous damage market hunting inflicted upon wildlife in North America during the nineteenth century and promises: "Never again!" Like all rules, this one invites exception. Some have argued that the virtual elimination of the legal ivory trade by treaty (the Convention on International Trade in Endangered Species, or CITES) has simply driven ivory poaching further underground, to the eventual detriment of the African elephant. These issues are too complex to argue here. But wildlife is still killed for commerce throughout the world with disastrous consequences, especially when it is taken for parts more valuable than the market price of its meat alone, as in the case of the black rhino and Bengal tiger.

These practices are not confined to Third World countries. When I visited Sweden in 1990 to watch my father receive the Nobel Prize in Medicine, I was startled to find moose hams and black grouse hanging all over the public market in Stockholm. When our hosts assured me that the "harvest" (this may be one case in which this euphemism for killing game is justified) was carefully regulated for the benefit of all concerned, including wildlife populations, I relaxed a little bit—but not much. I'm still more comfortable here, where such things just aren't done.

Wildlife should be managed according to democratic principles of law. The history of wildlife conservation in North America is founded on legal principle. Landmark legislation, almost always sponsored by sportsmen, sequentially established more and better legal safeguards for the benefit of wildlife and their habitat. Important court decisions in turn upheld their validity. All citizens had the right to participate in this process, by organizing into advocacy groups, helping to draft legislation, and supporting electoral candidates who shared their concern for wildlife. These opportunities continue today. Again, this principle may seem obvious to us, but it is by no means universal. In much of the world, crucial wildlife management decisions are made by private landowners (who may or may not have wildlife's best interests at heart), corrupt local authorities, or by no one at all.

All citizens have an equal right to hunt and fish. This is simply a reaffirmation of the democratic principles espoused by Grinnell, Roosevelt, and Leopold. All of them were astute enough to realize that in an egalitarian society, policies that reserve the enjoyment of wildlife (or any other public resource) for an elite group will eventually prove disastrous for the resource and its users alike.

Wildlife should not be killed without a valid reason. A wide body of law codifies this principle, defining, often in very specific terms, not only what reasons are valid but what the hunter must do in order to fulfill this obligation. Killing for food is the most widely accepted—and generally well-regarded—reason to kill a wild animal. "Wanton waste"—killing an edible game animal for some other reason (like trophy horns) without salvaging the meat—is a serious offense in most states. Alaska sets the standard on this issue, specifying exactly what portions of meat must be salvaged from a game animal (virtually everything edible) and prohibiting practices such as packing out trophy horns ahead of the last load of meat. Similar, if less comprehensive, statutes apply in most states to most game animals, with the notable exception of large predators.

Defense of life and property are also widely regarded as acceptable justifications for killing wild animals. Harvesting trophy horns alone is not. Surveys consistently show that the non-hunting public—the voting majority that will ultimately determine the future of hunting—is far more likely to approve of hunting when obtaining food is its primary purpose.

As hunters, we need to pay more attention to this principle. Some countries actually do a better job with this one than we do. Every possible scrap of every animal I've ever seen killed in Africa, for example, has been salvaged for eventual human consumption. In Australia and New Zealand, on the other hand, where all game animals derive from imported feral stock and are generally regarded as vermin, eating what you shoot is a principle more often honored in the breach than the observance.

Wildlife is an international resource. In our own legal history, this principle dates back to the 1918 Migratory Bird Treaty Act. The basic idea is simple enough: Wildlife doesn't carry passports or recognize international boundaries. It would be absolutely impossible for Americans to manage "our" waterfowl without the direct involvement of our neighbors in Canada and Mexico, as the leadership of Ducks Unlimited recognized early on. Our legislators wisely kept this principle in mind when they drafted the North American Wetlands Conservation Act and Wetlands Reserve Program. The international nature of the wildlife resource also defines the need for the CITES treaty. While some well-traveled sportsmen complain about its more onerous provisions, it's obviously impossible to act effectively against illegal worldwide trade in wildlife without operating at the international level.

Wildlife should be managed according to scientific principles. Our collective knowledge of wildlife biology has advanced qualitatively over the course of the last century. This expertise is hardly unique to North America. Wildlife managers in Europe and Africa, to cite two examples, bring an approach to the subject that's every bit as professional as our own. The distinction lies in what our respective societies choose to *do* with that knowledge. However, the gap between public policy and evidence-based scientific principles sometimes seems impossible to bridge. Emotionalism is the principal culprit, especially when combined with a political agenda. Examples abound: legislation that allows the destruction of delicate desert habitat by introduced feral horses at the expense of native wildlife; the altruistic but unreasonable preservationist impulse to make Yellowstone National Park support more bison than its natural carrying capacity ever allowed. While the NAWCM can't solve those political and societal dilemmas for us, it can articulate how they should be approached.

These principles have gained rapid and widespread acceptance among hunting and non-hunting wildlife advocates alike. The Rocky Mountain Elk Foundation, the Sierra Club, the Wildlife Society, and the Orion Institute, among others, cite them in their literature.

Of the seven, the first four do most to distinguish North American wildlife management from that in other countries. They're hardly new ideas—Grinnell, Roosevelt, and Leopold all stressed their importance years ago. And they work. As applied in the United States and Canada, they've given us healthy, free-ranging, unfettered populations of wildlife unequaled anywhere else in the world. Unfortunately, those four principles also seem to be the ones most immediately threatened today, not just in distant nations, but here at home where they have served wildlife so well.

"At the very core of the North American Wildlife Conservation Model," Steve Williams summarizes on behalf of the Wildlife Management Institute, "one finds that wildlife is a public resource. No individual, organization, business, or government owns wildlife . . . Public wildlife was intended to be available to all citizens, managed through science, free from commercial interests, and regulated in trust for future generations."

That is the mandate the next generation of sportsmen—and sportswomen—will have to respect if they are to continue the tradition of successful wildlife advocacy begun by Grinnell, Roosevelt, and Leopold.

AFTERWORD

"Wildlife conservation in North America has been premised on the principle that wildlife resources are owned by no one, and are held in trust by government for the benefit of present and future generations," according to John F. Organ of the U.S. Fish and Wildlife Service. "Indeed, the keystone pillar of the North American Model of Wildlife Conservation is that wildlife are public trust resources. Our model of wildlife conservation in North America has been hailed by many as the greatest example worldwide. Now that the legacy of this model is extending into its third century and nearly 150 years of history, one would think it is firmly entrenched. However, as the model reaches into this new millennium, its basic foundation is under siege."

What will the coming decades hold for sportsmen, wildlife, and their complex interrelationships? Will sportsmen successfully extend their proven record of advocacy on behalf of wildlife here and abroad? Will hunting and angling survive the obvious environmental and social challenges ahead?

If you were to ask a random sample of outdoorsmen to identify the gravest threat to the future of their sport, most hunters would almost certainly name the anti-hunting, animal rights movement. (Anglers should not feel complacent. Bringing a halt to recreational fishing is on the agenda of many of these groups as well.) Anti-hunting activists, who have learned to manipulate the media far more effectively than hunters, certainly cause their share of distress among sportsmen. Their emotionally driven arguments and the confrontational tactics they use to express them defy an essential tenet of the North American Model: Wildlife should be managed according to scientific principles.

In the battle for the hearts and minds of the 80 percent of the public who remain uncommitted toward hunting, the best counter is a rational explanation of sportsmen's true accomplishments on behalf of wildlife. Indeed, presenting that record for just this purpose was one of the driving impulses behind this book. But despite all the antagonism anti-hunting activists have aroused, their real impact on policy to date has been relatively minor. While I do not dismiss the threat they pose to sportsmen (and, paradoxically, to wildlife), I suggest that we need to order our priorities. As of yet, the anti-hunting movement does not belong at the top of the list of threats.

As Gordon Batcheller of the New York Division of Fish, Wildlife and Marine Resources argued in an analysis of hunting's future presented at the 2006 conference of the Western Association of Fish and Wildlife Agencies:

> We should not be overly concerned about anti-hunting
> organizations. There is no doubt that these groups have had
> isolated or even statewide impacts, some very significant, but
> I do not think they will have long-term negative consequences
> for hunting in the United States . . . These organizations will
> be very active and will be successful from time to time. They
> may have significant statewide effects on major programs,
> e.g., trapping or bowhunting. This will be frustrating
> and threatening. Wildlife agencies or non-governmental
> conservation organizations or both will be tempted to engage
> them in debate and conflict, expending a lot of money in the
> process and using important political capital as well. This may
> not be a prudent long-term strategy. The benefits will likely
> not exceed the costs.

Sportsmen and sportsmen's organizations have helped wildlife most when they've served as effective stewards of the environment and advocates of wildlife habitat. No concerned outdoorsman, hunter or non-hunter, should ever grow complacent about habitat, threats to which can only be expected to increase in the decades to come. Our government's failure to formulate a coherent energy policy will no doubt result in political pressure to relax environmental safeguards in increasingly desperate attempts to extract fossil fuels from sensitive areas critical to wildlife. The planet's human population will continue to expand, challenging wildlife for living space. The scientific evidence for climate change due to human activity is now conclusive. It will not even take a worst-case climate change scenario to produce an environmental crisis sufficient to make all other concerns irrelevant.

Traditional sporting values have undergone a relentless assault over the last several decades. Fixation upon "trophy quality" has concentrated attention on the results of the hunt rather than the process. Since we live in a market-driven, technology-rich society, abundant, commercially available resources have arisen to help provide shortcuts to those results. A generation of outdoorsmen is learning to tackle the outdoors with their credit cards and computers rather than woodsmanship skills. These trends reached a ludicrous extreme in the notorious case of the Texas "virtual deer hunt," in which a customer remotely fires a rifle at an actual deer using a video-equipped computer terminal.

As Batcheller noted in his 2006 analysis cited earlier:

> Newer and younger hunters will be shaped by the video
> and digital industry, expecting quick and easy results, and
> they will be infatuated with technology, at the expense of
> core skills and understanding of wildlife behavior. They will
> have unrealistic expectations of success. They will demand
> liberalization from state agencies . . . Generally, we are poor
> at anticipating technology and equally lacking in responding
> appropriately to the ethical conundrums often associated with
> technology. We should anticipate technology and the effects
> of these advancements on the hunting community and on
> society's perception of hunters and hunting. We should not
> accept technology without challenge, especially when these
> developments may harm the future of hunting.

Driven by advertising dollars, the outdoor media have bought into this new paradigm all too often. How frequently does one see pictures of honestly taken *cow* elk in hunting magazines? Of course, not all contemporary hunters and anglers have yielded to these pressures, but at the end of the day it's all too easy for a few to buy the results that they want at the expense of others.

The National Shooting Sports Foundation (NSSF) documented a decline in U.S. hunter numbers from some twenty-five million in 1987 to fifteen million in 2003, a drop of nearly 40 percent. That's ten million Americans who are no longer directly motivated by active participation in hunting to join sportsmen's wildlife advocacy groups, vote for policies favorable to wildlife and the places it lives, contribute financial and personal resources to habitat improvement, and otherwise engage in the kinds of pro-wildlife activities documented in the preceding chapters. Numerous factors have been proposed to explain this phenomenon, including the increasing urbanization of American society, the rise in single-parent households, and, of course, the anti-hunting movement. The fact remains that it's difficult for young Americans to become hunters when they have no place to hunt. And as Dr. Valerius Geist points out, "The most important thing sportsmen can do is multiply! We need numbers!"

Even hunters blind to the importance of sportsmen's historical involvement in conservation should be paying attention to these developments. In 2004 House of Commons Speaker Michael Martin invoked the Parliament Act for just the fourth time since 1949 to break a legislative deadlock and pass a bill banning fox-hunting with hounds in England. Blame (or credit) for this development largely fell upon anti-hunting activists, who were indeed their usual noisy selves during the debate. However, their true impact on the issue proved relatively minor. Foxhunting was correctly perceived as the exclusive province of the upper classes, and the British public simply saw no reason to maintain this privilege for the benefit of the wealthy few.

In its own way, the ban reflected the democratic principles of the NAWCM. When only the rich are able to enjoy hunting in America, hunting here may well suffer the same fate. As Dr. Geist notes, "Public hunting as we know it may not go on if the wealthy and political elite manage to de facto privatize wildlife and use it exclusively for their own pleasure."

Clearly, sportsmen still have work to do.

I refuse to conclude this project on a pessimistic note. In contrast to my previous collections of outdoor tales, this book involved real work, and I learned a lot in the process. What I learned frankly made me proud. I'm the first to acknowledge that sportsmen have made and continue to make errors in judgment, both as matters of individual conduct and public policy, and I've spent years trying to improve upon those shortcomings, both on my own part and others'. But a detailed review of the historical facts leaves me secure in my support of this book's original thesis: In sum, sportsmen have been highly beneficial to wildlife.

I continue to respect others' right to oppose hunting and fishing because they find these activities distasteful, and I even continue to respect others' right to oppose hunting and fishing because they find them immoral. But I do not accept anyone's right to oppose these activities on the grounds that they are detrimental to wildlife and the environment. The facts prove otherwise, and the world deserves to know it.

ORGANIZATIONS

As an indication of the success sportsman-driven conservation and habitat organizations enjoy today, there are simply too many to review in the body of the text. There are even too many to list here, and I apologize to those worthwhile groups I've omitted because of their focus on narrow regional concerns or inadvertent oversight on my part. However, the following roster will help provide a starting point for readers interested in obtaining more information or offering their support to the worthy causes these organizations represent. The groups listed are either sportsman-driven or have shown a willingness to work with sportsmen on conservation issues.

Aldo Leopold Foundation, www.aldoleopold.org

American Fisheries Society, www.fisheries.org

American Prairie Foundation, www.americanprairie.org

American Rivers, www.americanrivers.org

American Sportfishing Association, www.asafishing.org

Atlantic Salmon Federation, www.asf.ca

Billfish Foundation, www.billfish.org

Boone and Crockett Club, www.boone-crockett.org

Coastal Conservation Association, www.joincca.org

Delta Waterfowl Foundation, www.deltawaterfowl.org

Ducks Unlimited, www.ducks.org

Federation of Fly Fishers, www.fedflyfishers.org

Fish America Foundation, www.fishamerica.org

Foundation for North American Wild Sheep,
   www.wildsheepfoundation.org

International Game Fish Association, www.igfa.org

International Hunter Education Association, www.ihea.org

Izaak Walton League of America, www.iwla.org

J. N. (Ding) Darling Foundation, www.dingdarling.org

Mule Deer Foundation, www.muledeer.org

National Bowhunter Education Foundation, www.nbef.org

National Wild Turkey Federation, www.nwtf.org

National Wildlife Federation, www.nwf.org

Outdoor Writers Association of America, www.owaa.org

Pheasants Forever, www.pheasantsforever.org

Pope and Young Club, www.pope-young.org

Professional Bowhunters Society, www.bowsite.com/pbs

Quail Unlimited, www.qu.org

Rocky Mountain Elk Foundation, www.rmef.org

Ruffed Grouse Society, www.ruffedgrousesociety.org

Theodore Roosevelt Conservation Partnership, www.trcp.org

Trout Unlimited, www.tu.org

Western Association of Fish and Wildlife Agencies,
www.wafwa.org

Wildlife Society, www.wildlife.org

BIBLIOGRAPHY

Arseniev, V. K. *Dersu the Hunter*. New York: Dutton, 1941.

Bakeless, John, ed. *The Journals of Lewis and Clark*. New York: Penguin, 1964.

Benson, W. Todd. *President Theodore Roosevelt's Conservation Legacy*. Haverford, PA: Infinity Publishing, 2003.

Bergman, Charles. *Orion's Legacy*. New York: Dutton, 1996.

Clark, Marvin H. *Last of the Great Brown Bear Men*. Spokane, WA: Great Northwest Publishing, 1980.

Corbett, Jim. *Man-Eaters of India*. New York: Oxford University Press, 1957.

Cutright, Paul Russell. *Lewis and Clark: Pioneering Naturalists*. Lincoln, NE: University of Nebraska Press, 2003.

Dayton, Duncan, and Ken Burns. *Lewis and Clark*. New York: Knopf, 1997.

Dickson, James G., ed. *The Wild Turkey: Biology and Management*. Mechanicsburg, PA: Stackpole Books, 1992.

Dolan, Eric Jay, and Bob Domaine. *The Duck Stamp Story*. Iola, WI: Krause, 2000.

Jolma, Dena. *Hunting Quotations*. Jefferson, NC: McFarland & Co., 1992.

Jones, Allen Morris. *A Quiet Place of Violence*. Bozeman, MT: Spring Creek Press, 1997.

Jones, Robert. *African Twilight*. Bozeman, MT: Wilderness Adventure Press, 1994.

Kerasote, Ted. *Bloodties*. New York: Random House, 1993.

Kraft, Betsy Harvey. *Theodore Roosevelt*. New York: Clarion, 2003.

Lee, Richard, and Irven Devore, eds. *Man the Hunter*. New York: Aldine de Gruyter, 1968.

Lendt, David. *The Life of Jay Norwood Darling*. Ames, IA: University of Iowa Press, 1979.

Leopold, Aldo. *Game Management*. New York: Scribner's, 1933.

———. *A Sand County Almanac*. New York: Oxford University Press, 1949.

Lonner, Terry, and Harold Picton. *Montana's Wildlife Legacy*. Bozeman, MT: Media Works, 2008.

Lott, Dale E. *American Bison: A Natural History*. Berkeley, CA: University of California Press, 2002.

Lund, Thomas A. *American Wildlife Law*. Berkeley, CA: University of California Press, 1980.

McPhee, John. *The Founding Fish*. New York: Farrar, Straus and Giroux, 2002.

Meine, Curt. *Aldo Leopold*. Madison, WI: University of Wisconsin Press, 1998.

Mitchell, John. *The Hunt*. New York: Knopf, 1980.

Morris, Edmund. *Theodore Rex*. New York: Random House, 2001.

Mussehl, Thomas W., and F. W. Howell, eds. *Game Management in Montana*. Helena, MT: Montana Fish and Game Department, 1971.

Ortega y Gasset, Jose. *Meditations on Hunting*. Bozeman, MT: Wilderness Adventure Press, 1995. First published in 1942 by Scribner.

Peacock, Doug, and Andrea Peacock. *The Essential Grizzly*. New York: Lyons Press, 2006. New York.

Petersen, David. *Ghost Grizzlies*. Boulder, CO: Johnson Books, 1998.

Philbrick, Nathaniel. *Mayflower*. New York: Penguin, 2006.

Posewitz, Jim. *Beyond Fair Chase*. Helena, MT: Falcon, 1994.

———. *With Rifle in Hand*. Helena, MT: Riverbend, 2004.

Punke, Michael. *Last Stand*. New York: Harper Collins, 2007.

Quammen, David. *Monster of God*. New York: W. W. Norton, 2003.

Reiger, John F. *American Sportsmen and the Origins of Conservation.* Norman, OK, and London: University of Oklahoma Press, 1986.

Roosevelt, Theodore. *African Game Trails.* New York: Charles Scribner's Sons, 1910.

Schullery, Paul. *The Bear Hunter's Century.* New York: Dodd, Mead, 1988.

Shields G. O. *Hunting in the Great West.* Chicago: Belford, Clarke, 1882.

Street, Bill, ed. *2004 Conservation Directory.* Washington, D.C.: Island Press, 2004.

INDEX

on conservation, 97
in Conservation
    Commission, 105
"Conservation Ethic" by, 103
creating NMGPA, 99
essays by, 105–7
forest fires and, 100–101
as forester, 98
founding Wilderness
    Society, 104
founding Wildlife Society,
    104, 105
Game Management by, 102
on habitats, 102
"Land Ethic" by, 106
policy dispute of, 161
on predator control, 100,
    101, 193
Round River by, 97
Sand County Almanac by,
    104, 107
saving waterfowl and, 89
teaching Game Management,
    104, 106
on wolves, 192
working for Forest Products
    Laboratory, 101
working for Forest Service, 98,
    99, 100
working for SAAMI, 101, 102
Lewis, Meriwether. *See* Lewis and
    Clark expedition
Lewis and Clark expedition, 15–17
antelopes and, 111
elk and, 114, 115
Native Americans and, 16, 17
observing prairie habitat,
    156, 157
wild turkeys and, 6
See also Corps of Discovery
Lilly, Ben, 191
Little Ice Age, 20–21

lobbies, 49, 51, 53–54, 55
Ludlow, William, 49, 50

M

Mackenzie, Alexander, 120
Maneaters of India (Corbett), 179
Manifest Destiny, 27, 69
Marsh, Othneil, 48
Martin v. Waddell, 204
Massachusetts Zoological and
    Botanical Survey, 19
Mather, Cotton, 34
Maximilian, Prince, 6
MBTA (Migratory Bird Treaty Act),
    84–87, 167, 207
McKinley, William, 67, 68, 82
McNeir, Forest, 127–28
McPhee, John, 27
Merriam, C. Hart, 114
Mineral Land Act, 69
Monster of God (Quammen), 193
Mooar, J. Wright, 21
More Game Birds in America
    Foundation, 95, 96
Morton, Thomas, 13
mourning dove, 39
Muir, John, 35, 69, 70, 71, 72

N

National Bison Range, 119
National Conference of
    Governors, 76
National Geographic, 85
National Reclamation Act, 68, 69
National Wildlife Federation, 93,
    96, 97
National Wildlife Refuge System,
    75, 78, 90
Native Americans
depending on bison, 20,
    23–24, 50
horses influencing, 21

red drum fish, 130–33, 137
rhinos, 176, 178
rivers, damming, 27, 28
RMEF (Rocky Mountain Elk
    Foundation), 143–45, 159,
    161, 207
Robertson, A. Willis, 93
Roosevelt, Franklin Delano, 89
Roosevelt, Theodore
    in Africa, 172
    African Game Trails by, 77, 184
    background of, 66
    Boone and Crockett Club and,
        59–60, 67
    Bull Moose Party and, 75
    convening National Conference
        of Governors, 76
    creating national monuments, 74
    creating wildlife refuges, 74–75
    Elk Horn Ranch of, 65
    on Forest Service, 69
    Grinnell and, 52, 53–54, 59, 72
    Hunting Trips of a Ranchman by,
        52, 59, 67
    Pastimes of an American Hunter
        by, 72
    political career of, 66–67
    as President, 68, 77
    protecting birds, 76
    protecting seals, 76
    Rough Riders and, 67
    as Secretary of the Navy, 67
    as sportsman, 73
    supporting Adirondacks
        conservation, 67
    supporting bison, 119
    supporting conservation, 47,
        64, 68
    supporting national parks, 74
    supporting Yellowstone National
        Park, 53, 61–62
    "Teddy Bear" story of, 73–74

    Theodore Roosevelt Conservation
        Partnership and, 150–53
    Round River (Leopold), 97
    Royal Customs Service, 13
    Russia, 179–83

S
SAAMI (Sporting Arms and
    Ammunition Manufacturers'
    Institute), 101
Saltern, Felix, 11
Sand County Almanac (Leopold),
    104, 107, 192
Schullery, Paul, 191
Schuylkill Navigation Company, 27
Secretary of the Interior, 52, 53, 63
selective citation, 14
Senate Committee on Conservation
    of Wildlife Resources, 89
Seton, E. T., 14
shad, American
    colonists depending on, 15,
        25–26
    commercial harvest of, 25–28
    habitat of, 28
    population decline of, 25–28
    Samuel Howell on, 26
    Schuylkill Navigation Company
        affecting, 27
    Seth Green on, 28
    spawning of, 27
    Washington on, 26
Sheridan, Phil, 23–24
Shiras, George III, 85, 86
Sierra Club, 137, 151, 207
Silent Spring (Carson), 11
Singer, Peter, 11
Slater, William, 141
Smith, John, 25
Spanish-American War, 67
sporting clubs, 45–46, 54
    influencing habitats, 45–46

ABOUT THE AUTHOR

In addition to writing about outdoor sports and wildlife, E. Donnall Thomas Jr. works as a physician on a remote Montana Indian reservation and as a hunting guide in Alaska, where he has also been a pilot and a commercial fisherman. He and his wife Lori, a registered nurse and photographer, divide their time between homes in both states. He is the co-editor of *Traditional Bowhunter* and Field Editor for *Ducks Unlimited* and *Retriever Journal*, and his work appears regularly in publications such as *Gray's Sporting Journal, Pheasants Forever, Alaska, Bowhunter, Fish Alaska, Shooting Sportsman*, and numerous other national publications. He has won the Traver Award for fly-fishing fiction and his stories have appeared in many anthologies.